STAR WARS

EPISODE II

ATTACK OF THE CLONES

STAR WARS ™

Published by Pedigree Books Limited
Beech Hill House, Walnut Gardens, Exeter, Devon EX4 4DH.
E-mail books@pedigreegroup.co.uk
Published 2005

£7.99

TIMELINE

YEAR	
-19	Vader and Obi-Wan duel on Mustafar
-19	Luke & Leia born
-19	Death of Padmé Amidala
-4	Lando loses the *Falcon* to Han
-2	Corellian Treaty
0	Alliance steals Death Star plans
0	**STAR WARS: A NEW HOPE**
0	Obi-Wan shows Luke the Force
0	Emperor dissolves Senate
0	Destruction of Alderaan
0	Death of Obi-Wan
0	Battle of Yavin
0	Destruction of the Death Star
3	**THE EMPIRE STRIKES BACK**
3	Battle of Hoth
3	Luke trains on Dagobah
3	Han Solo frozen in carbonite
3.5	Boba Fett delivers Solo to Jabba
4	**RETURN OF THE JEDI**
4	Death of Jabba the Hutt
4	Death of Yoda
4	Battle of Endor
4	Death of the Emperor
4	Redemption of Anakin Skywalker
4	Destruction of Death Star II

JEDI ARCHIVE

C-3PO

This talkative protocol droid, built by Anakin Skywalker, is fluent in several million forms of communication. Anakin spent long hours in Watto's junkyard, scavenging for parts to build him. C-3PO is inclined to worry but is a loyal servant.

R2-D2

R2-D2 is a brave astromech droid. He has a wide range of built-in tools, which he uses to repair vehicles and other machinery. He is also an excellent navigator and is designed to operate in deep space. He communicates in an electronic language of beeps, chirps and whistles.

YODA

Jedi Master Yoda is greatly respected for his wisdom and insight and for his strong connection to the Force. He is one of the most experienced members of the Jedi Council and is over 800 years old. Yoda's skill with a lightsaber is second to none on the Council.

DARTH SIDIOUS

Darth Sidious is an evil Sith Lord who wants to destroy the Jedi order and expand his own power. His true identity is a mystery, but his growing power will have dramatic effects on the entire galaxy. Darth Sidious plots for galactic domination and secretly creates interplanetary strife to threaten the Republic.

COUNT DOOKU

Count Dooku is a fallen Jedi – a disciple of the dark side and a fierce warrior. He has always wielded considerable power – by natural authority, by lightsaber, and now by wealth and persuasion. Dooku was seduced to the dark side by Darth Sidious, the Dark Lord of the Sith.

IDENTITY FILES

JANGO FETT

After his parents were killed, Jango Fett was adopted and raised by the Mandalorian warrior army. The Jedi destroyed this dangerous force, but Fett survived and continues to wear the armoured, weapon-filled uniform that helped make the Mandalorians a dreaded name.

ANAKIN SKYWALKER

Anakin Skywalker is gifted with extraordinary Force skills and piloting abilities. His talents make him impatient with Jedi traditions that seem to hold him back and he often disagrees with the more cautious Obi-Wan Kenobi.

PADMÉ AMIDALA

Padmé Amidala is dedicated to the safety and peace of her home planet, Naboo. She is a strong-willed young woman and a gifted politician, who believes in democracy and speaks out against war.

OBI-WAN KENOBI

A dedicated Jedi Knight, Obi-Wan Kenobi is heavily influenced by the teachings of many leading Jedi, including Yoda. Obi-Wan is a quick, agile and bold warrior. He is also extremely resourceful and trustworthy.

PALPATINE

Chancellor Palpatine presents himself as a mild-mannered servant of the public good, avoiding ostentation and always protecting the limits of his abilities.

SHIPS AND MACHINES

AT-TE

DESCRIPTION:	ALL TERRAIN TACTICAL ENFORCER ASSAULT WALKER
SIZE:	13.2M LONG
SPEED:	60KPH
WEAPONS:	6 LASER CANNON TURRETS, 1 HEAVY PROJECTILE CANNON
CREW/ PASSENGERS:	1 PILOT, 1 SPOTTER, 4 GUNNER/SUPPORT CREW, 1 EXTERIOR GUNNER

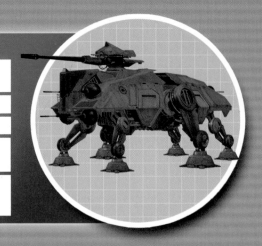

SOLAR SAILER

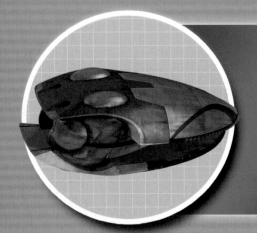

DESCRIPTION:	PUNWORCCA 116-CLASS INTERSTELLAR SLOOP
SIZE:	16.8M LONG
SPEED:	1,600KPH
WEAPONS:	84 NARROW-BEAM TRACTOR/REPULSOR EMITTERS
CREW/ PASSENGERS:	1 DROID PILOT, 1 OPTIONAL COPILOT

GEONOSIAN FIGHTER

DESCRIPTION:	NANTEX-CLASS TERRITORIAL DEFENCE STARFIGHTER
SIZE:	9.8M LONG
SPEED:	20,000KPH
WEAPONS:	1 LASER CANNON TURRET
CREW/ PASSENGERS:	1 PILOT

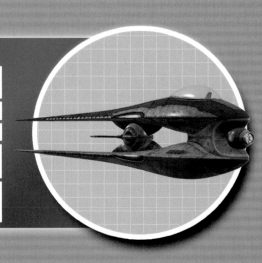

REPUBLIC ASSAULT SHIP

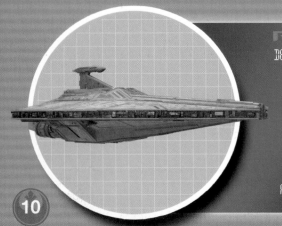

DESCRIPTION:	ACCLAMATOR-CLASS TRANS-GALACTIC MILITARY TRANSPORT SHIP
SIZE:	752M LONG
SPEED:	3500G
WEAPONS:	12 QUAD TURBOLASER TURRETS, 24 LASER CANNONS, 4 MISSILE/TORPEDO LAUNCH TUBES
CREW/ PASSENGERS:	700 CREW

TRADE FEDERATION CORE SHIP

DESCRIPTION:	LUCREHULK-CLASS MODULAR CONTROL CORE
SIZE:	696M DIAMETER
SPEED:	300G
WEAPONS:	280 POINT-DEFENCE LIGHT LASER CANNONS
CREW/ PASSENGERS:	60 SUPERVISORS, 3,000 DROID CREW, 200,000 MAINTENANCE DROIDS

BONGO

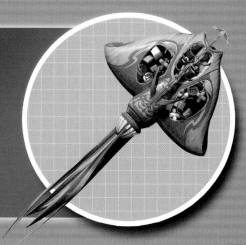

DESCRIPTION:	GUNGAN UNDERWATER CRAFT
SIZE:	15M LONG
SPEED:	85KPH
WEAPONS:	NONE
CREW/ PASSENGERS:	1 PILOT + 2 PASSENGERS

NABOO ROYAL STARSHIP

DESCRIPTION:	J-TYPE 327 CHROMIUM-COVERED STARSHIP
SIZE:	76M LONG
SPEED:	920KPH
WEAPONS:	NONE
CREW/ PASSENGERS:	1 PILOT, 1 COPILOT + UP TO 6 ADDITIONAL CREW MEMBERS, 8 ASTROMECH DROIDS FOR REPAIR AND MAINTENANCE

REPUBLIC CRUISER

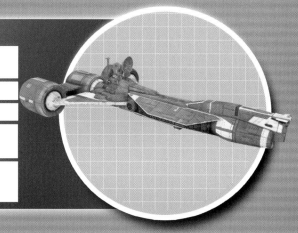

DESCRIPTION:	STARSHIP FOR CARRYING AMBASSADORS ON DIPLOMATIC MISSIONS
SIZE:	115M LONG
SPEED:	900KPH
WEAPONS:	NONE
CREW/ PASSENGERS:	8 CREW + 16 PASSENGERS

SITH INFILTRATOR

DESCRIPTION:	DARTH MAUL'S PERSONAL STARSHIP WITH CLOAKING DEVICE
SIZE:	26.5M LONG
SPEED:	1,180KPH
WEAPONS:	6 CONCEALED LASER CANNONS
CREW/ PASSENGERS:	1 PILOT + UP TO 6 PASSENGERS

ASTROMECH

QUI-GON JINN

Qui-Gon Jinn was trained by Count Dooku. Now a wise Jedi Master, Qui-Gon is strongly connected to the living Force. He has great compassion and empathy for other living things, and is an accomplished warrior.

Greed and political scheming are weakening the Republic that Qui-Gon serves. In an attempt to restore lasting peace and security to the galaxy, Qui-Gon is motivated to take a more active role than that traditionally taken by the Jedi.

Jedi robe

Jedi tunic

Lightsaber

Utility belt

Rugged travel boots

Hairless skull

Face tattoos

Horns

Yellow eyes

Double-bladed lightsaber

DARTH MAUL

Darth Maul is a relentless Sith warrior who employs the powers of the dark side to serve Darth Sidious. His face is a mask of bizarre tattoos. Sharp horns form a crown around his bald head, and his ferocious eyes reveal a spirit twisted by rage.

Maul's lightsaber contains two sets of internal components and his Sith infiltrator spaceship is equipped with a rare cloaking device, allowing him to travel invisibly.

HOLO FILES

Amphibious head

Protruding eyes

Duck-like snout

Broad flat ears

JAR JAR BINKS

Jar Jar Binks is a Gungan from the vast underwater city of Otoh Gunga. He speaks in a dialect and always seems to be just one step away from trouble. Jar Jar is very kind and helpful, but rather clumsy and strange. His trusting nature can be easily exploited by dishonest people.

3 fingers and a thumb on each hand

Rubbery body

Enhanced breath filter for battle conditions

Comlink antenna built into helmet

Utility belt carries spare blaster magazines, survival gear and assault equipment

DC-15 blaster

CLONE TROOPER

Clone troopers are identical in appearance, intelligence and stamina. They are grown in the cloning facilities of Kamino, where their genetic structure has been altered to make them less independent.
Clone trooper armour is based on the battle gear of the Mandalorian supercommando. Together with their superb training and conditioning, clone troopers feel virtually invincible.

EPISODE 1
THE PHANTOM MENACE

The Galactic Republic is in turmoil. The greedy Trade Federation has stopped all shipping to the small planet of Naboo by putting a blockade of starships around the planet.

Supreme Chancellor Valorum has secretly sent two Jedi Knights, the guardians of peace and justice in the galaxy, to settle the conflict.

Master Qui-Gon Jinn and his Padawan, Obi-Wan Kenobi, arrive at the blockade. When Gunray realises the ambassadors are Jedi Knights, he is frightened. Gunray contacts Lord Sidious, a mysterious figure in a hooded cloak that hides his face. He orders the Viceroy to kill the Jedi Knights.

Droids are sent to do the job, but Jedi cannot be killed so easily! Qui-Gon and Obi-Wan destroy the droids and rush to the landing platform, but their ship has been destroyed. They see vast numbers of battle droids and realise it is an invasion army. They must warn Queen Amidala of Naboo.

Qui-Gon and Obi-Wan stow away on battle ships and are carried down to Naboo. On the planet they meet a Gungan called Jar Jar Binks, who takes them to the hidden Gungan city to ask for help. But the Gungan leader, Boss Nass, refuses to aid the Naboo people. With Jar Jar, the Jedi make a dangerous and frightening journey through the planet core to the Naboo capital city.

The Trade Federation army captures the Queen, but the Jedi and Jar Jar Binks rescue her and her handmaidens. With the help of a droid called R2-D2 they escape Naboo on a cruiser and set a course for Coruscant. The Queen hopes the Senate will stop the Trade Federation.

When the Viceroy tells Lord Sidious that Queen Amidala has vanished, he sends his Sith apprentice Darth Maul to find her.

The cruiser's hyperdrive is leaking and they have to stop to refuel and repair the ship. They land on Tatooine, which is controlled by gangsters called the Hutts. Qui-Gon takes Jar Jar Binks, R2-D2 and a handmaiden called Padmé to a nearby settlement to find parts for the ship.

A dealer called Watto has the parts they need, but they have no money. Watto's assistant is a young slave boy called Anakin Skywalker. He introduces them to his mother, Shmi, and his droid, C-3P0, which he built himself.

He thinks Padmé is very beautiful and tells her that he is a pilot. He has built a Podracer and is the only human who is quick enough to compete in the dangerous sport. He offers to help Qui-Gon by entering the Boonta Eve Classic Podrace and using the prize money to buy parts.

Qui-Gon senses that there is something special about Anakin. The Force is unusually strong with him. He discovers that the boy's midi-chlorian count is the highest ever known.

Meanwhile a ship lands on Tatooine and Darth Maul steps out. He sends probe droids across the sandy wasteland.

Qui-Gon makes a deal with Watto that if Anakin wins, he will be set free. He tries to free Anakin's mother too, but Watto will not risk losing two slaves.

Vast, cheering crowds have come to the arena to see the Boonta Eve Classic. Qui-Gon advises Anakin not to think, but just to use his instincts. Padmé and Shmi watch as the vile Jabba the Hutt starts the race.

It is dangerous – many competitors crash and explode into balls of flame. It needs quick reflexes and agility. A cheat called Sebulba tries to knock Anakin out of the race, but Anakin gets into first place on the final lap.

Sebulba crashes as Anakin whizzes over the finish line and wins!

The cruiser is repaired and Anakin sadly says goodbye to his mother. He is keen to train as a Jedi, but he finds it hard to leave her behind. He says goodbye to C-3P0 and promises to come back one day and free his mother.

Before Qui-Gon can get on the cruiser, he is attacked by Darth Maul. They whirl and duel on the sands of Tatooine, until Qui-Gon leaps onto the cruiser and they speed away, leaving the furious Darth Maul behind.

Senator Palpatine, the Naboo representative in the Senate, meets them at Coruscant. Palpatine tells the Queen that the Senate is full of greedy, squabbling delegates. The Supreme Chancellor has no real power. He suggests getting a stronger Supreme Chancellor by calling for a vote of no confidence in Chancellor Valorum.

The Queen addresses the Senate and moves for a Vote of No Confidence. Palpatine is nominated as a candidate for the new Supreme Chancellor and the Queen decides to return to Naboo to be with her people.

Qui-Gon reports to the Jedi Council that his attacker was a Sith Lord. Master Mace Windu can hardly believe it, as the Sith have been extinct for a millennium, but Master Yoda reminds him that the dark side is hard to see. Qui-Gon also tells the Council about Anakin.

He thinks Anakin is the prophesied Chosen One who will bring balance to the Force. Qui-Gon wants to train him to be a Jedi. The Council tests Anakin but they feel that he thinks about his mother too much. He fears to lose her, and fear is the path to the dark side. They refuse to train the boy.

Qui-Gon is amazed and vows to train Anakin himself. The Jedi Council promises to discuss it again, but for now Qui-Gon and Obi-Wan must return to Naboo with the Queen. They have to discover the identity of the dark warrior. Secretly, the mysterious Lord Sidious also sends Darth Maul to Naboo.

The Queen's ship lands on Naboo and Jar Jar Binks takes her to see Boss Nass. Suddenly Padmé steps forward and reveals that she is really Queen Amidala! She has been using a decoy to fool her enemies. She begs Boss Nass for his help and he agrees.

Padmé draws up her battle plans. The Gungans will draw the droid army away from the capital city with a decoy battle. Padmé will lead a strike team into the city and capture the Viceroy. They will also send pilots into space to knock out the droid control ship that is orbiting the planet.

The Gungans march on the droid army and the battle begins as Padmé and her team creep into the city. They burst into the landing area and the Naboo pilots take off in their fighters. Qui-Gon tells Anakin to hide and the boy climbs into the cockpit of a spare fighter with R2-D2.

Droidekas roll into the hangar and start firing. Darth Maul appears and ignites a double-bladed lightsaber. His red eyes glow with evil and he launches himself on Qui-Gon and Obi-Wan.

Anakin turns his fighter on the droidekas and turns it on. He shoots them down and Padmé escapes with her team, but Anakin's fighter is now on automatic pilot! It zooms up into space to join the battle against the droid control ship.

Padmé and her team race through the palace to the throne room, where they capture the Viceroy. Outside the city, the Gungans fight bravely but there are hundreds of thousands of droids and they are hopelessly outnumbered.

Darth Maul leads the Jedi onto a narrow bridge, jumping and twisting as he attacks them. He throws Obi-Wan off the bridge and continues to fight Qui-Gon. It is a mighty duel, but Darth Maul is too fast – he plunges his lightsaber into Qui-Gon's stomach.

"No!" cries Obi-Wan. He pulls himself up and rushes towards Darth Maul.

The Gungans call a retreat, but they are surrounded by battle droids. In space, R2-D2 manages to get the fighter out of autopilot and Anakin flies into the droid control ship. He shoots at the main reactor and the droid ship starts to lose power. Anakin escapes as it explodes into tiny pieces. On Naboo, all the droids stop working and the Gungans are safe! Obi-Wan is a powerful fighter, athletic and fast.

At last he cuts the evil Sith in half with his lightsaber and rushes to Qui-Gon's side. With his last breath, Qui-Gon makes Obi-Wan promise to train Anakin as a Jedi.

Palpatine has been made Supreme Chancellor and promises to bring peace and prosperity to the Republic. Obi-Wan is made a Jedi Knight and the Jedi Council agrees to let Anakin be his Padawan learner. But Yoda fears grave danger in his training.

Beside Qui-Gon's funeral pyre, Mace Windu and Yoda quietly discuss the Sith. There are only ever two – a master and an apprentice. The apprentice has been destroyed – but who is the master?

EPISODE 2
ATTACK OF THE CLONES

It is ten years since the Trade Federation's attack on Naboo and there is unrest in the Galactic Senate. Several thousand solar systems have declared their intentions to leave the Republic.

This Separatist movement, under the leadership of the mysterious Count Dooku, has made it difficult for the small number of Jedi Knights to maintain peace and order in the galaxy.

Senator Padmé Amidala, the former Queen of Naboo, returns to the Galactic Senate to vote against creating an Army of the Republic.   But when her cruiser lands on Coruscant, it is blown up. The Senator dies, but she is a decoy! The real Padmé is in a fighter disguised as a guard.

Padmé is placed under the protection of Master Obi-Wan Kenobi and his Padawan learner, Anakin Skywalker. Obi-Wan and Anakin meet Padmé and Jar Jar Binks again after ten years. Anakin is attracted to Padmé, but she still thinks of him as a little boy.

A helmeted figure meets a hired assassin called Zam Wesell. She reports that she failed to kill Senator Amidala. He gives her some poisonous creatures and she sends a droid to put them into Padmé's bedroom.

Obi-Wan and Anakin stand guard outside Padmé's bedroom as she sleeps. When the droid puts the creatures into the room they sense danger and rush in. Anakin kills the creatures while Obi-Wan leaps through the window and clings to the droid. It speeds through the air to Zam, who shoots it, sending Obi-Wan tumbling down! But Anakin is behind him on a speeder and catches him.

They chase Zam Wesell through the busy streets of Coruscant and finally catch her in a club. She is about to tell them the name of the bounty hunter who hired her, when she is shot dead with a toxic dart. The Jedi see her helmeted killer fly away with a rocket pack on his back.

The Jedi Council orders Obi-Wan to track down the bounty hunter, while Anakin is told to escort Padmé back to Naboo and protect her. Obi-Wan does not think Anakin is ready for this assignment because he is too arrogant, but Mace Windu and Yoda do not listen to him. They believe that Anakin is the Chosen One who will bring the Force back into balance.

Padmé leaves with Anakin for Naboo. As they travel, he tells her about being a Jedi and how he feels that Obi-Wan is holding him back. Padmé begins to see that Anakin is no longer a child.

Obi-Wan discovers that the toxic dart that killed Zam comes from Kamino, a planet beyond the Outer Rim. Kaminoans are skilled cloners. He searches the archive charts for Kamino but it has been erased from the archive's memory. This is worrying because only a Jedi could have erased the files.

Obi-Wan flies to Kamino, an ocean planet. To his amazement, they are expecting him. He is taken to meet the Prime Minister, Lama Su. Lama Su tells Obi-Wan that they have created a vast clone army for the Republic. He thinks that the Jedi Council ordered this army years ago.

Obi-Wan hides his surprise and asks to see the army. As he is shown the hundreds of thousands of clone troopers, he learns that the original host is a bounty hunter called Jango Fett. Apart from his pay, Jango demanded an unaltered clone for himself, which he is bringing up as his son. Obi-Wan suspects that Jango is the bounty hunter who has been trying to kill Senator Amidala.

On Naboo, Padmé and Anakin have grown very close. Anakin uses his Jedi skills to show off to her and he tells her that he has fallen deeply in love with her. But a Jedi is not allowed to love. Padmé tells him that their love can never be because she could not live a lie. He knows that she is right and admits that it would destroy them.

That night Anakin has a terrible nightmare about his mother, Shmi. He realises that she is in danger and decides to return to his home planet of Tatooine, even though he is disobeying the Jedi Council's orders. Padmé goes with him and they set off in a cruiser with R2-D2.

Obi-Wan transmits a report to Yoda and Mace Windu. They are shocked to hear about the clone army and order him to bring Jango Fett in for questioning. Obi-Wan fights with Jango Fett, but the bounty hunter manages to get away with his son.

Obi-Wan throws a homing device onto the hull of Jango's ship and follows him into space. Anakin and Padmé arrive on Tatooine. They discover that Shmi was sold to a moisture farmer called Cliegg Lars, who freed her and married her. But when they find the Lars homestead, they discover that Shmi has been captured by Tusken Raiders. Anakin goes to hunt for her.

Obi-Wan follows Jango to a planet called Geonosis. Count Dooku is there with Nute Gunray, the Viceroy of the Trade Federation. They have created a huge army of battle droids. They think that it will be the greatest army in the galaxy. The Jedi will be overwhelmed and the Republic will agree to anything.

Obi-Wan tries to transmit a message to Anakin and discovers he is now on Tatooine.

He starts to send the message, but he is seen by a Geonosian creature!

On Tatooine, Anakin reaches the Tusken Raiders' camp and finds his mother, but he is too late. She has been beaten and is almost dead. She tells Anakin she loves him before dying in his arms. Anakin is overcome with grief. He turns on the Tusken Raiders and ignites his lightsaber, his face dark with rage and hatred.

Anakin returns to the Lars homestead with his mother's body. He has slaughtered the Tusken Raiders – men, women and children. At his mother's graveside, he promises never to fail again. He vows to become the most powerful Jedi ever.

R2-D2 shows Anakin and Padmé the report from Obi-Wan. They start to transmit it to the Jedi Council, but Obi-Wan is attacked halfway through his message. Anakin and Padmé disobey the Jedi Council and go to Geonosis to help Obi-Wan.

The Senate grants Palpatine emergency powers so that he can make instant decisions about this threat to the Republic. Now he has complete control, but he promises to lay down the power when the crisis is over. He announces that they will use the clone army to fight the Separatists.

When Padmé and Anakin arrive on Geonosis they are captured and condemned to death. Padmé tells Anakin that she loves him and they kiss. They are led into the execution arena where they see Obi-Wan.

Dooku, Jango Fett and the other Separatist leaders watch as three terrible beasts are pushed into the arena.

Padmé, Obi-Wan and Anakin fight bravely and overpower the beasts, but then they are surrounded by droidekas! It looks as though they are beaten, but suddenly a cloaked figure appears and holds a lightsaber to Jango Fett's throat. It is Mace Windu!

All around the arena, Jedi Knights pull off their cloaks and ignite their lightsabers. Dooku calls his droids into the arena and an almighty battle begins between the droids and the Jedi.

Mace leaps into the arena and fights back to back with Obi-Wan. Anakin and Padmé chop down hundreds of droids. Mace lops off Jango Fett's head as Boba watches in horror. Yoda sweeps out of the sky with a fleet of gunships and clone troopers!

Soon the droid army is in full retreat. The Separatists are afraid that the Jedi will find their designs for an ultimate weapon. Count Dooku takes the designs and sets off on a speeder, planning to deliver them to his master.

Obi-Wan sees Count Dooku escaping and follows him with Anakin. Dooku flies to a hangar where a spaceship is waiting for him, but Anakin and Obi-Wan are close behind.

Anakin and Obi-Wan fight Count Dooku bravely, but Dooku is better. With a terrible laugh he defeats Obi-Wan and chops Anakin's arm off. Anakin falls to the ground next to Obi-Wan. Count Dooku thinks he has won. But then he hears someone else walking into the hangar. It is Yoda!

Dooku and Yoda duel so fast they are like blurs in the dark hangar. But Count Dooku cannot defeat Yoda, and he is exhausted. He uses the Force to make a huge crane fall towards Anakin and Obi-Wan. Yoda has to stop it!

It takes all Yoda's strength to hold the crane off. Count Dooku runs to his ship and escapes. Next morning he is greeted by the evil and mysterious Darth Sidious. He is very pleased. Everything has gone exactly as they had planned!

Anakin gets a new mechanical arm and takes Padmé home to Naboo, where they get married in secret.

Supreme Chancellor Palpatine gives orders for thousands of clone troopers. He watches as they march into battle ships, to be sent to all corners of the galaxy. Yoda is very worried.

"The shroud of the dark side has fallen," he warns Obi-Wan. "Begun the Clone War has."

C-3PO Quiz

An intelligent protocol droid like me has to have a lot of information at his fingertips. These questions will test many aspects of your knowledge. Answer them and let's find out just how smart you are!

1

We are surrounded by destroyer droids! We have to tap in the launch code for the starship before they start shooting. Can you work out what the last number will be?

1 1 2 21 31

2

Look at these badges. Can you match each badge with the person who wears them?

a) Empire b) Rebellion c) Jango Fett d) The Sith

1.   2.   3.   4.

3

When we arrived on Geonosis, my head got stuck on the wrong body in the droid foundry. It is all very confusing. Can you work out which head belongs on which body?

1.   2.   3.   4.

4

Padmé is in terrible danger. She is trapped in the droid foundry. She can only move forwards when the metal stampers are up. Can you work out the pattern and tell her if the next machine will be up or down?

5

The Separatists have scrambled our communicators and we cannot understand any messages. Can you unscramble these words to make a sentence?

AYM TEH ROCEF EB HWIT UYO

6

I am familiar with six million forms of communication. These are some words from alien languages. Can you rearrange the letters to make some important names?

1. DOAY   _ _ _ _

2. NINAKA   _ _ _ _ _ _

3. MEDPA   _ _ _ _ _

4. AECM NIDUW   _ _ _ _ _ _ _ _ _

5. GAJON TEFT   _ _ _ _ _ _ _ _ _

6. NTUOC ODUKO   _ _ _ _ _ _ _ _ _ _

7

How many square starships can you create from these shapes?

Now count your scores. Give yourself one point for every correct answer. Then check your intelligence levels below.

1-3 – Oh my! You know even less than R2-D2!

4-6 – Most impressive. Your circuits must be in excellent working order.

7 – Are you a Jedi, by any chance?

27

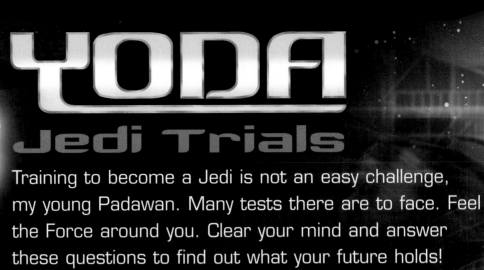

YODA
Jedi Trials

Training to become a Jedi is not an easy challenge, my young Padawan. Many tests there are to face. Feel the Force around you. Clear your mind and answer these questions to find out what your future holds!

1

You sense a major disturbance in the Force. What do you do?

a. Find the source of the disturbance and destroy it.
b. Ask the High Council what they would like you to do.
c. Ignore it. There is probably nothing you can do about it.

2

You have cornered a Jedi who has turned to the dark side. You know that he may be a better fighter than you. What do you do?

a. Run back to the Jedi Council – there is no point in getting yourself killed.
b. Pull out your lightsaber. If he attacks, you will be ready.
c. Attack him before he attacks you. You fly at him with your lightsaber.

3

What is your most important possession?

a. Your calm and peaceful unity with the Force. Material possessions mean nothing to you.
b. The lightsaber that you constructed yourself.
c. Your photographs of your family back at home.

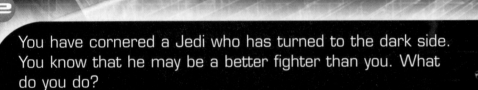

4

You sense that your family is in danger, but the Jedi Council has ordered you to stay where you are. What do you do?

a. Ignore the Council's orders and return home.
b. Obey the Council and try to bury your feelings.
c. Explain what you have sensed to the Council and ask for their advice.

5

Even a young Padawan knows that the power of the Force is all around. How do you feel about it?

a. You call upon it with great respect. It is not a toy – it is the greatest power in the galaxy.
b. You believe that it should be used for fun as well as for serious issues.
c. You can see what its power can do and you wish to control it.

6

You are chasing a villain but you lose them. What do you do?

a. Stay calm and use the Force to find them again.
b. Go back to the Council and apologise for failing.
c. Lose your temper and carry on looking. You will find them if it takes all night!

Count up your scores and add them to your previous totals. There are more tests to come before you reach the level of Jedi Knight.

①	②	③
a. 6	a. 2	a. 10
b. 10	b. 10	b. 6
c. 2	c. 6	c. 2

④	⑤	⑥
a. 6	a. 6	a. 6
b. 10	b. 10	b. 10
c. 2	c. 2	c. 2

STAR WARS™
EPISODE III
REVENGE OF THE SITH

Episode III

REVENGE OF THE SITH

It is a time of great unrest. Since the Battle of Geonosis three years ago, the Clone Wars have raged across the galaxy, with the massive Jedi-led clone army of the Republic fighting the droid army of the Separatists. The Galactic Republic has begun to crumble under the stress of war. Already, the Jedi have suffered many casualties as Masters and Padawans fall during the struggle to restore order. Some citizens are beginning to doubt whether the Jedi really have the best interests of the galaxy in mind. Many citizens are being swayed to think that the Jedi are acting for their own goals.

Supreme Chancellor Palpatine has gained enough support from those within the Senate to take almost-absolute power. The Senate has grown increasingly corrupt. The Jedi Council fears that the Sith are plotting to overthrow the Republic itself, since the existence of Darth Sidious was revealed to Obi-Wan Kenobi. While many clues have been uncovered, the Jedi have yet to expose Darth Sidious and bring him to justice.

The Republic is crumbling under attacks by the ruthless Sith Lord, Count Dooku. There are heroes on both sides. Evil is everywhere. In a stunning move, the fiendish droid leader, General Grievous, has swept into the Republic capital and kidnapped Chancellor Palpatine, leader of the Galactic Senate. As the Separatist Droid Army attempts to flee the besieged capital with their valuable hostage, two Jedi knights lead a desperate mission to rescue the captive Chancellor...

PADMÉ AMIDALA

Three years after Padmé Amidala secretly wed Anakin Skywalker, the beautiful young Senator is hiding both her marriage and her pregnancy from those around her. She is consumed with anxiety and fear over the dangers of the war and the fate of the crumbling Republic.

DARTH SIDIOUS

After plotting for years to take over the Republic, the evil Darth Sidious prepares to seize his chance. Now, when the Republic is vulnerable and the Jedi are overwhelmed, he is ready to unleash his reign of terror upon the galaxy.

OBI-WAN KENOBI

In the years since the beginning of the Clone Wars, Obi-Wan Kenobi has served as a general in the ongoing war against the Separatists and has become a Jedi Master. He and Anakin have been fighting bravely in the Outer Rim sieges for five months.

BAIL ORGANA

Senator Bail Organa of Alderaan is a trusted advisor in Chancellor Palpatine's inner circle. He sees that the Senate has become hopelessly corrupt, but he is determined not to let a thousand years of democracy disappear without a fight.

PALPATINE

Supreme Chancellor Palpatine continues to preside over the Galactic Senate as the Clone Wars rage on. He tightens his grip on the Senate and masses ever-greater powers, determined to fight until the war is won.

IDENTITY FILES

R2-D2

R2-D2 is assigned to serve Anakin Skywalker in the Clone Wars, seated in the droid socket of Anakin's Jedi starfighter. R2-D2's ingenuity and spirit prove invaluable as he accompanies his master on dangerous missions throughout the galaxy.

ANAKIN SKYWALKER

After three years on the front lines of the Clone Wars, Anakin Skywalker's incredible feats have made him a hero throughout the Republic and earned him full Jedi Knight status. Anakin continues to conceal his marriage to Padmé, and has not seen her for several months.

MACE WINDU

A member of the Jedi Council and a fearsome warrior, Mace Windu believes that action must be taken before democracy and freedom are completely stripped from the Republic. He is respected for his profound wisdom and remarkable accomplishments. Mace Windu is never afraid to stand in the face of danger.

YODA

While the Clone Wars ravage the galaxy, Yoda is concerned by the growing disturbance in the Force and the deteriorating situation in the crumbling Republic. He leads the Republic's clone army into battle, assisted by the mighty Wookiees Chewbacca and Tarfful.

KI-ADI-MUNDI

Ki-Adi-Mundi is a thoughtful Cerean, with a binary brain supported by a second heart. He was trained in the Jedi arts by Jedi Master Yoda himself and is a member of the Jedi Council. He has been made a Republic general in the Clone Wars because of his keen insight and natural leadership abilities.

SHIPS AND MACHINES

REPUBLIC ATTACK GUNSHIP

DESCRIPTION:	LAAT/I (LOW-ALTITUDE ASSAULT TRANSPORT/INFANTRY) REPULSORLIFT GUNSHIP
SIZE:	17.4M LONG
SPEED:	620KPH
WEAPONS:	3 ANTI-PERSONNEL TURRETS, 2 MASS-DRIVER MISSILE LAUNCHERS, 4 COMPOSITE-BEAM PINPOINT LASER TURRETS, 8 LIGHT AIR-TO-AIR ROCKETS
CREW/ PASSENGERS:	1 PILOT, 1 COPILOT/GUNNER, 2 AUXILIARY TURRET GUNNERS CARRIES 30 CLONE TROOPERS, 1 IM-6 BATTLEFIELD MEDICAL DROID (STOWED IN EMERGENCY LOCKER).

TRADE FEDERATION MTT

DESCRIPTION:	ARMOURED REPULSORLIFT VEHICLE USED TO TAKE BATTLE DROIDS INTO COMBAT
SIZE:	31M LONG
SPEED:	35KPH
WEAPONS:	NONE
CREW/ PASSENGERS:	2 PILOT BATTLE DROIDS AND 2 ADDITIONAL BATTLE DROIDS CARRIES 112 BATTLE DROIDS ON STORAGE RACK

JEDI STARFIGHTER

DESCRIPTION:	DELTA-7 AETHERSPRITE LIGHT INTERCEPTOR; SYLIURE-31 LONG-RANGE HYPERDRIVE MODULE
SIZE:	8M LONG
SPEED:	12,000KPH
WEAPONS:	2 DUAL LASER CANNONS
CREW/ PASSENGERS:	1 PILOT, 1 MODIFIED, INTEGRATED ASTROMECH DROID

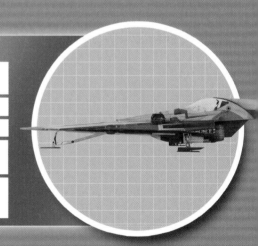

TRADE FEDERATION BATTLESHIP

DESCRIPTION:	A TRADE FEDERATION FREIGHTER CONVERTED TO SERVE AS A WEAPON OF WAR
SIZE:	3,170M DIAMETER
SPEED:	300G
WEAPONS:	42 QUAD LASER EMPLACEMENTS
CREW/ PASSENGERS:	CARRIES 1,500 DROID STARFIGHTERS, 50 C-9979 LANDING SHIPS, 550 MTTS, 6,250 AATS, 1,500 TROOP CARRIERS

TRADE FEDERATION LANDING SHIP

DESCRIPTION:	TRADE FEDERATION STARSHIP DESIGNED TO TRANSPORT MACHINES AND TROOP CARRIERS TO A PLANET'S SURFACE
SIZE:	370M WINGSPAN
SPEED:	587KPH
WEAPONS:	4 TURRET-MOUNTED CANNONS AND 2 PAIRS OF WING-TIP LASER CANNONS
CREW/ PASSENGERS:	88-DROID CREW, CARRIES 28 TROOP CARRIERS, 114 AATS, 11 MTTS

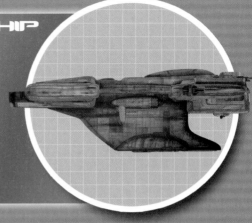

ANAKIN'S AIRSPEEDER

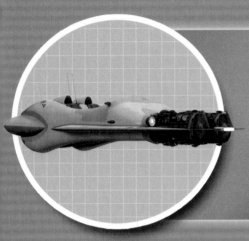

DESCRIPTION:	UNIQUE, CUSTOM-BUILT LUXURY HOT ROD
SIZE:	6.23M LONG
SPEED:	720KPH
WEAPONS:	NONE
CREW/ PASSENGERS:	1 PILOT + 1 PASSENGER

PADMÉ'S STARSHIP

DESCRIPTION:	CUSTOMISED H-TYPE NUBIAN YACHT
SIZE:	47.9M LONG
SPEED:	8,000KPH
WEAPONS:	NONE
CREW/ PASSENGERS:	1 PILOT, 1 COPILOT, 2 OPTIONAL (NAVIGATOR, COMSCAN/SHIELD OPERATOR), 2 ASTROMECH DROIDS

WHEEL BIKE

DESCRIPTION:	GENERAL GRIEVOUS'S TSMEU-6 PERSONAL WHEEL BIKE WITH ALTERNATE WALKING MODE
SIZE:	2.5M DIAMETER
SPEED:	330KPH
WEAPONS:	DOUBLE LASER CANNON
CREW/ PASSENGERS:	1

CHEWBACCA

The Wookiee warrior Chewbacca serves under the command of Jedi Master Yoda in the Clone Wars, when Separatist forces invade his homeworld of Kashyyyk. Chewbacca can tear the limbs off most creatures barehanded and his weapon of choice is a bowcaster, a crossbow-like weapon that shoots explosive packets of energy. A bandolier slung from his shoulder contains enough extra firepower to take on a squad of stormtroopers.

Hair

Bandolier

Bag

Gold-coloured eyes with reptilian pupils and blood-red sockets

Six fingers on each hand

4 victims' lightsabers

Hardened alloy armour

GENERAL GRIEVOUS

The supreme commander of the droid armies and a brilliant military strategist, General Grievous leads the forces of the Confederacy into battle against the crumbling Republic. Part alien, part droid, he hunts Jedi for sport and proudly displays his victims' lightsabers around his belt as trophies. He has no compassion or scruples and his unorthodox fighting style, strategic ingenuity and flawless cunning make him almost invincible.

Heavy shoulder armour

Main signal receptor unit

SUPER BATTLE DROID

The Trade Federation's defeat in the Battle of Naboo made it clear that they needed stronger, more independent infantry forces, so the super battle droids were commissioned. Their thick acertron armour protects the primary power unit and their cryogenically tempered body shell elements are hardened, but flex slightly under stress to reduce breakage.

Handtip contains firing impulse transmitter

Tranlang III communications module

Monogrip hands

AA1 VerboBrain

Strap-on foot tips can be replaced with claws or pads depending on the terrain

Fragile inner wiring

Gold coverings given in service of Padmé

C-3PO

During the Clone Wars, C-3PO serves Padmé Amidala loyally, staying with her during her darkest moments. As the servant of a Senator, he wears gold coverings. He remains faithful to the Skywalker family, together with his companion R2-D2, during the political turmoil of the time.

37

REVENGE OF THE SITH

Obi-Wan Kenobi and Anakin Skywalker lead an assault against General Grievous's starship in near space above Coruscant's surface. The Jedi dodge incoming laser fire and are attacked by a host of Separatist forces, including vulture droid fighters and droid tri-fighters. "General Grievous's ship is directly ahead!" shouts Anakin. Suddenly, Obi-Wan's starfighter is attacked by buzz droids.

Anakin tries to blast them off, but Obi-Wan's ship is disintegrating. He crashes onto the hangar bay of General Grievous's command ship.

"R2-D2, locate the Chancellor!" orders Obi-Wan.

After fighting their way through battle droids, Obi-Wan and Anakin reach the main room of Grievous's quarters and find Palpatine shackled to a chair.

"Are you all right?" asks Anakin. But just then, Count Dooku strides into the room with two super battle droids.

"You won't get away this time, Dooku!" says Obi-Wan as he and Anakin ignite their lightsabers. A great swordfight begins. Obi-Wan and Dooku grow tired, but Anakin becomes stronger as he gets angry. Count Dooku throws Obi-Wan back using the Force. He falls to the lower level, unconscious.

"I sense great fear in you, Skywalker," says Dooku. "You have hate, you have anger, but you don't use them."

Anakin attacks with a new ferociousness and finally cuts off Count

Dooku's hands. Dooku stumbles to the floor.

"Kill him! Kill him now!" urges Palpatine. Anakin cuts off Count Dooku's head.

With laser fire still rocking the command ship, Anakin hoists Obi-Wan up onto his shoulders. Together with the Chancellor, he heads for the hangar bay to escape the severely damaged ship. Obi-Wan

regains consciousness and they reach the hangar. Just then, General Grievous activates the ship's ray shields, which drop around the Jedi and trap them.

They are escorted to the bridge where they find R2-D2 and are brought before General Grievous.

"Ah, Jedi scum," says the general. "Your lightsabers will make a fine addition to my collection."

"Not this time," says Obi-Wan. "And this time you won't escape."

Another battle erupts as Anakin and Obi-Wan engage more super battle droids as well as Grievous and his bodyguards. During the fight, alarms signal that the cruiser has begun falling out of orbit. Grievous rushes to the escape pod bay. After jettisoning every other pod, he launches himself into space,

leaving Obi-Wan, Anakin, and Palpatine trapped aboard the crashing ship!

The only hope for survival is to safely land the badly damaged cruiser on Coruscant. As the others strap themselves in, Anakin sits at the helm and reaches out with the Force to help steady the ship and keep the hull from burning up. With fire ships flanking them, the young Jedi is able to guide the smoking wreck down to the planet's surface, where he makes a hard landing near an industrial platform.

Back on Coruscant, the Chancellor, Obi-Wan and Anakin are met by a group of senators.

"Chancellor Palpatine, what a welcome sight!" says Mace Windu. "Are you all right?"

"Yes, thanks to your two Jedi Knights," replies Palpatine.

Obi-Wan returns to the Jedi Temple, while Anakin accompanies Palpatine, Bail Organa and the senators to the Republic Senate building. At the back of the crowd, Anakin and Organa talk quietly.

"The end of Count Dooku will surely bring an end to this war, and an end to the Chancellor's security measures," says Organa.

"I wish that were so," says Anakin. "But the fighting is going to continue until General Grievous is spare parts."

Behind a row of large columns, a shadowy figure follows Organa and Anakin as they talk. Anakin senses this figure and excuses himself. It is his wife, Padmé Amidala.

"Oh, Anakin!" cries Padmé as they embrace.

"I missed you, Padmé," says Anakin, overjoyed to hold his wife again.

"There were whispers ... that you'd been killed," Padmé continues.

"I'm all right," Anakin smiles. "It feels like we've been apart for a lifetime. And it might have been... If the Chancellor hadn't been kidnapped. I don't think they would have ever brought us back from the Outer Rim sieges."

Anakin starts to give her another kiss, but she steps back.

"Wait, not here..." she says, afraid that

they will be seen.

Anakin grabs her again. "Yes, here! I'm, I'm tired of all this deception. I don't care if they know we're married!"

"Anakin, don't say things like that!" Padmé cries.

Anakin looks at her then embraces her again. "Are you all right?" he asks suddenly. "You're trembling. What's going on?"

Padmé is nervous and excited. "Something wonderful has happened," she says. "I'm pregnant."

Anakin is happy about the news, but Padmé is worried. She and Anakin have kept their vows a secret. If the Jedi Council ever found out that he was about to become a father, they would expel Anakin from the order. But Anakin takes her in his arms again.

"We're not going to worry about anything right now, all right? This is a happy moment. The happiest moment of my life."

Meanwhile, a Neimoidian shuttle lands on the sinkhole planet of Utapau. General Grievous steps onto the landing platform, surrounded by a group of super battle droids. He is led to the grand chambers of the Separatist Council. The hologram of a hooded figure appears in the room. General Grievous immediately bows to the shimmering image of the Sith Lord, Darth Sidious.

"The end of the war is near, General," says Lord Sidious.

"But the loss of Count Dooku?"

"His death was a necessary loss, which will ensure our victory," says Lord Sidious. "Soon I will have a new apprentice… one far younger and more powerful than Lord Tyranus."

On Coruscant, Padmé and Anakin share a wonderful evening together. They enjoy being back together and make plans to raise their child on Padmé's home planet of Naboo. But that night, Anakin has dreams of his wife dying in an alien medical chamber during childbirth. He awakens from the nightmare in a panic and leaves the room.

Padmé joins him on the large veranda.

"What's bothering you?" asks Padmé.

"It was a dream," says Anakin slowly. "Like the ones I used to have about my mother just before she died."

"And?"

"It was about you. You die in childbirth."

"It was only a dream," says Padmé. "Anakin, this baby will change our lives. I doubt the Queen will continue to allow me to serve in the Senate, and if the Council discovers you are the father, you will be expelled from the Jedi order."

"I know," sighs Anakin.

"Do you think Obi-Wan might be able to help us?" asks Padmé.

Anakin is suspicious. "He's been a father to me," he says. "But he's still on the Council. Don't tell him anything. I don't need

his help… our baby is a blessing, not a problem."

The following day, Anakin meets with Yoda to tell him about his dreams. He does not reveal that they are about Padmé – only that only that they are about someone close him. Yoda listens with concern.

"Careful you must be when sensing the future, Anakin. The fear of loss is a path to the dark side."

"I won't let these visions come true, Master Yoda."

"Death is a natural part of life," says

Yoda. "Attachment leads to jealousy. The shadow of greed, that is. Train yourself to let go of everything you fear to lose."

Anakin leaves the meeting to join Obi-Wan. Something is troubling the older Jedi. Obi-Wan explains that the Senate is expected to vote more powers to the Chancellor. Anakin is happy with this news, believing that the decision will make it easier to end the war. But Obi-Wan is

sceptical about Palpatine.

"Anakin, be careful of your friend Palpatine," he says. He then informs his young apprentice that the Chancellor has asked to see Anakin without telling the Jedi Council why. Obi-Wan feels very uneasy about the request because relations between the Council and the Chancellor are strained.

"The Force grows dark," he says. "Be wary of your feelings."

Anakin goes to see Palpatine.

"This afternoon the Senate is going to call on me to take direct control of the Jedi Council," says the Chancellor. "They will report to me personally."

Palpatine tells Anakin that he is proud of his achievements, and that he hopes Anakin will trust him. He asks for Anakin's help, claiming that he fears the Jedi and saying that they are shrouded in secrecy.

The Chancellor appoints young Skywalker as his representative on the Jedi Council; he wants Anakin to be the eyes, ears, and voice of the Republic. Anakin is thrilled by the honour, but he doesn't think the Council will accept his appointment.

Later, in Bail Organa's office, a group of senators are discussing the fact that the Chancellor now has control of the Jedi Council.

"We can't let a thousand years of democracy disappear without a fight," says Organa. "It has become increasingly clear that the Chancellor has become an enemy of democracy."

"I can't believe it has come to this!" exclaims Padmé.

The senators agree to do what they can to stop the Chancellor. They also agree to keep their plans a secret – even from their own families.

Anakin goes before the Council, where his appointment as the Chancellor's personal representative is approved. But the Jedi are suspicious of Palpatine's motives and refuse to give Anakin the title of 'Master'. Anakin loses his temper.

"This is outrageous!" he yells. "I'm more powerful than any of you!"

The other Jedi are embarrassed by his outburst. Anger, pride, and lack of self

control are not part of a true disciple of the Force.

"Take a seat, young Skywalker," says Mace Windu quietly.

Anakin apologises and sits down, but deep inside he is furious. He believes that his deeds on the battlefield have more than earned him the right to the title of 'Master'.

After the meeting, Obi-Wan tells Anakin why the Council has accepted his appointment. The Jedi have grown increasingly suspicious of the Chancellor's true motives.

"The Council wants you to report on all of the Chancellor's dealings," Obi-Wan explains. "They want to know what he's up to."

Anakin is upset that the Council want him to spy on his good friend and mentor, but Obi-Wan asks him to search his feelings, to realise that something is out of place and to honour the Council's request.

Obi-Wan reports to Mace and Yoda that Anakin is unhappy about his new assignment.

"Too much under the sway of the Chancellor, he is. Much anger there is in him. Too much pride in his powers."

"I don't trust him," says Mace.

"With all due respect, Master, is he not the Chosen One?" asks Obi-Wan. "Is he not to destroy the Sith and bring balance to the Force?"

"A prophecy that misread could have been," says Yoda gravely.

"He will not let me down," Obi-Wan insists. "He never has."

Later, Anakin arrives at the Galaxies Opera House, where the Chancellor has requested a meeting. When the young Jedi enters the Chancellor's private box, Palpatine tells him that clone intelligence units have located General Grievous on the planet Utapau.

The Chancellor tells his aides to leave, and then leans in close to Anakin. Palpatine says that he can no longer rely on the Council.

"The Jedi Council wants control of the Republic," he tells Anakin. "They're planning to betray me."

"I know they don't trust you. I have to admit my trust in them has been shaken."

The Chancellor is happy to hear this. He goes on to say that the Jedi point of view is not the only true one, and that the Dark Lords of the Sith also believe in security and justice.

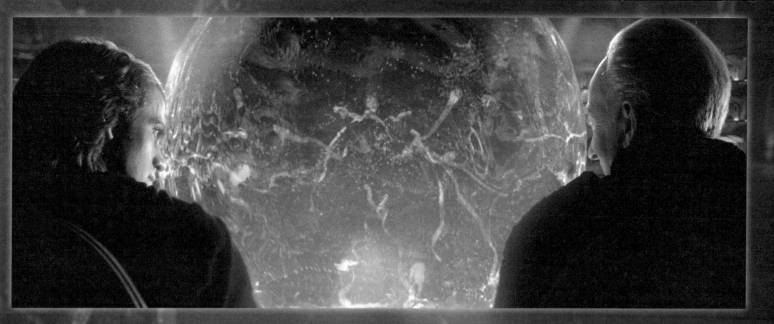

"The Sith and the Jedi are similar in almost every way," he says, "including their quest for greater power. The difference between the two is that the Sith are not afraid of the dark side of the Force. That is why they are more powerful."

Anakin is confused, because he has always been taught the Jedi are selfless and use their power only to help others, while the Sith are selfish, using their powers only to help themselves. But Palpatine says this isn't true. He tells Anakin about Darth Plagueis, a Sith Lord who was powerful and wise.

"He had such a knowledge of the dark side that he could even keep the ones he cared about from dying," says Palpatine.

Haunted by his dreams of Padmé dying, Anakin is intrigued by what the Chancellor is saying.

"He could actually save people from death?" he asks.

"The dark side of the Force is a pathway to many abilities some consider to be unnatural."

"Is it possible to learn this power?"

"Not from a Jedi," says Palpatine.

When the Jedi learn that Grievous is hiding on Utapau, they decide to act quickly.

Anakin wants to lead the campaign, but Mace Windu recommends sending a single Jedi, Master Kenobi. Anakin is angry. After the rest of the Council agree with the idea, Obi-Wan assembles two clone brigades to help him on his mission.

Next morning, Anakin and Obi-Wan walk onto a landing platform overlooking a docking bay. Thousands of clone troops, armoured weapons and tanks are being loaded onto a massive Republic Assault Ship.

"You're going to need me on this one, Master," says Anakin. He wants to accompany Obi-Wan to Utapau to find General Grievous.

"Oh, I agree," smiles Obi-Wan. "However, it may turn out just to be a wild bantha chase."

Obi-Wan turns to leave but Anakin calls after him. "Master!"

Obi-Wan stops and Anakin walks over to him.

"I've disappointed you," Anakin says sadly. "I haven't been very appreciative of your training. I have been arrogant and I apologise... I've just been so frustrated with the Council."

"You are strong and wise, Anakin, and I am very proud of you," replies Obi-Wan. "I have trained you since you were a small

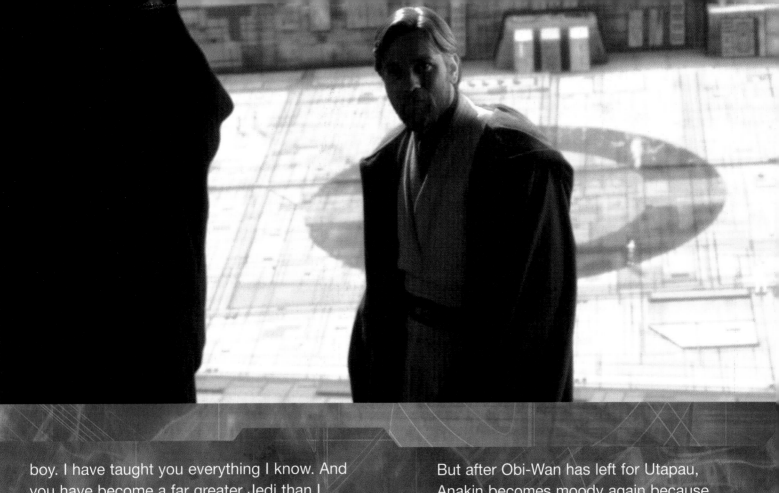

boy. I have taught you everything I know. And you have become a far greater Jedi than I could ever hope to be. But be patient, Anakin. It will not be long before the Council makes you a Jedi Master."

Obi-Wan again turns to leave.

"Obi-Wan, may the Force be with you!" Anakin calls out.

"Good-bye, old friend. May the Force be with you," replies Obi-Wan. Then he heads down a ramp towards the waiting Republic cruiser as Anakin watches him go.

But after Obi-Wan has left for Utapau, Anakin becomes moody again because he doesn't think Obi-Wan and the Council trust him. Anakin knows that something is happening to him. He's one of the most powerful Jedi, yet he still isn't satisfied. Still haunted by nightmares of Padmé dying during childbirth, Anakin explains to her that he has found a way to save her life, and that he is becoming more powerful with his new knowledge of the Force.

In his Jedi starfighter, Obi-Wan emerges from hyperspace and approaches the planet Utapau. When he arrives he is greeted by the local administrator, Tion Medon.

"I should like some fuel for my ship and to use the city as a base as I search nearby systems for General Grievous," he says. But Tion Medon draws close and quietly tells Obi-Wan that they are being held hostage by the general. Grievous and thousands of battle droids are stationed on the tenth level.

Obi-Wan instructs Tion Medon to tell his people to take shelter and his warriors to prepare for battle. He then returns to his

starfighter and tells his astromech droid, R4-G9, that he is staying on the planet and to take off and tell Commander Cody that he has made contact.

After watching his fighter leave, Obi-Wan makes his way through the city and comes across a corral filled with dragon-like lizards. Using the Force, Obi-Wan influences a nearby wrangler to give him transportation. Obi-Wan then hops on the lizard's back and they begin to climb up to the tenth level.

Obi-Wan finds Grievous standing

charge into the control centre, guns blazing.

"You must realise you are doomed!" says Grievous.

"I don't think so!" replies Obi-Wan. He continues his attack on Grievous and uses the Force to hurl the general backwards and onto the platform below. Obi-Wan begins to cut down battle droids as he spots Grievous racing toward one of the landing platforms.

He sees the general jump onto a wheel scooter and take off down the wall of the sinkhole. Obi-Wan jumps onto the lizard's back and goes after Grievous, dropping his lightsaber as he gives chase.

before the Council of Separatists. Grievous tells the Council that it will only be a matter of time before their enemies know where they are hiding. He sends them to the Mustafar system in the Outer Rim. After they leave, Obi-Wan follows the general to the control centre and makes his move. The general commands his bodyguards to attack the Master Jedi, but they are no match for him. Igniting his lightsaber, Obi-Wan easily parries the bodyguards' clumsy blows, cuts down one, and then uses the Force to bring the roof down on the rest.

"Back away. I will deal with this Jedi slime myself," snarls Grievous.

General Grievous's arms separate into four appendages and he grabs four lightsabers from his belt. He attacks Obi-Wan in a flashing display of swordsmanship, driving him all the way across the control centre. Obi-Wan mounts a counter-attack as battle droids begin firing on him.

Suddenly, dozens of clone troopers

On Coruscant, Clone Commander Cody reports to the Jedi Council that Obi-Wan is engaged in combat with Grievous, and that the troops have begun their attack. Mace Windu instructs Anakin to

Once Anakin has gone, Ki-Adi-Mundi suggests that they have the Chancellor removed from office if he does not give up his emergency powers. The Jedi discuss this, while Yoda warns that this line of

return to the Senate Building and deliver the report to the Chancellor, believing that Palpatine's reaction to the news will reveal his true intentions.

thinking will lead them to a very dark place. After a long chase through the city, Obi-Wan catches up with Grievous and jumps off his lizard and onto the general's bike, knocking them both to the ground.

Grievous fires on Obi-Wan with his blaster. The Jedi calls upon the Force, grabs the general's electrostaff, spins, and blocks the incoming bolts. Obi-Wan charges Grievous, swinging the staff and hitting the general in the stomach, knocking his gun away. Grievous pulls the Jedi close to him and the two engage in hand-to-hand combat.

Noticing that his stomach plate is loose, Obi-Wan rips it off and sees a bag that contains Grievous' organic innards.

The general grabs Obi-Wan and hoists him over his head, tossing him across the platform. As Obi-Wan dangles off the edge, Grievous grabs his electrostaff and charges the Jedi. At the last second, Obi-Wan reaches out with the Force to grab the general's blaster and fires it into Grievous's stomach, watching as his enemy explodes from the inside out.

Obi-Wan pulls himself up onto the platform and walks by the destroyed carcass.

"So uncivilised," he murmurs.

When he hears that Grievous has been found, Palpatine plants more seeds of doubt in Anakin's mind.

"Be careful of the Jedi," he says. "They fear you. In time they will destroy you. Let me train you."

Palpatine tells Anakin that he can teach him the subtleties of the Force that can help him break through the fog of lies the Council has created. He states that he knows the nature of the dark side.

"You know the dark side?" exclaims Anakin. Astounded, he presses Palpatine for more answers. At last the Chancellor reveals that he can teach Anakin the ways of the dark side, which will help him to save Padmé's life.

Anakin can't believe what he's hearing!

"You're a Sith Lord!" he shouts. He ignites his lightsaber, while Palpatine continues to bombard him with doubt, urging the young Jedi to follow his lead.

"I can feel your anger," he says. "It gives you focus, makes you stronger." Anakin raises his lightsaber to Palpatine's throat, then relaxes and turns off his weapon.

"I am going to turn you over to the Jedi Council," he says.

As Mace Windu and three Jedi board a gunship to the Chancellor's office, Anakin approaches them and says that he believes Palpatine is the Sith Lord they've been searching for.

"How do you know this?" asks Mace.

"He knows the ways of the Force," replies Anakin. "He has been trained to use the dark side."

Anakin asks if he can go with the Jedi to the Chancellor's office, but Mace refuses.

"There is much fear that clouds your judgement," he says. "If what you told me is true, you will have gained my trust, but for now remain here."

At the Senate Building, Mace and three Jedi enter the Chancellor's office, lightsabers ignited.

"In the name of the Galactic Senate of the Republic, you are under arrest, Chancellor," says Mace.

Palpatine brandishes his own lightsaber and spins towards them, cutting down all but Mace. The two battle fiercely, fighting their way down the hallway and into the main office. Palpatine uses the Force to slam Windu against a wall, but the Jedi recovers before the Chancellor can cut him down. Mace breaks the window behind the Chancellor's desk, and the two move out onto the ledge and fight over the precipice.

Meanwhile Anakin has been struggling with his feelings. He believes that if Palpatine dies, he will lose all chance of saving Padmé. At last he rushes out of the Council Chamber to his speeder. Anakin arrives just in time to see Mace knock Palpatine's lightsaber out of his hand.

"The oppression of the Sith will never return!" says Mace. "Your plot to regain control of the Republic is over. You have lost!"

Palpatine becomes enraged, shooting bolts of lightning out of his hands at Mace, which the Jedi blocks with his lightsaber. Mace pushes Palpatine right to the edge of the ledge, and as the Jedi moves closer, the bolts of lightning begin to arch back toward the Sith Lord. Palpatine's face starts to twist and distort, and his eyes become yellow as he struggles to intensify his powers. The Chancellor begs for his life, but Mace seems determined not to let him get away.

"You can't kill him, Master," cries Anakin. "He must stand trial."

"He is too dangerous to be kept alive!" insists Mace.

"It is not the Jedi way…" says Anakin, confused. "He must live… I need him." He thinks of Padmé. "NO!"

JOURNEY TO THE DARK SIDE

Anakin Skywalker never knew a father; rumours said that maybe the Force itself had brought him into being. Whatever the truth, he was destined to become one of the most famous and the most feared figures in the history of the galaxy.

Even as a boy, Anakin was strongly in tune with the Force and could sense events before they happened. Anakin had been a slave from the day he was born. He and his mother lived on Tatooine and were owned by a merchant named Watto. Resourceful, intuitive, and competitive, he was an excellent Podracer and very compassionate. When Qui-Gon Jinn landed on Tatooine needing help, Anakin was keen to volunteer, and he met Padmé Amidala for the first time.

Qui-Gon sensed the boy's strong connection to the Force. He believed that Anakin was the Chosen One of an ancient prophecy, and that he would one day bring balance to the Force.

Qui-Gon freed Anakin and took him away from Tatooine, although the boy found it difficult to leave his mother behind. This was the first sign of the weakness that would one day lead him to the dark side – he was too afraid of loss.

When Qui-Gon was killed by a Sith lord, Obi-Wan Kenobi took Anakin on as his Padawan. But Supreme Chancellor Palpatine, leader of the Republic, also took an interest in this unusual boy. For years, Palpatine fed Anakin's ego with whispered words of praise. Soon, the Chosen One felt he could do anything.

Under the guidance of Obi-Wan Kenobi, Anakin became a confident, headstrong young man with an impulsive nature and a flair for adventure. But his feelings for Padmé began to challenge his Jedi vows.

Anakin's first real step along the path to the dark side came when he finally returned to Tatooine. He discovered that his mother had been kidnapped by Tusken Raiders. Anakin travelled to the Tusken camp to find her, but she died in his arms. In his grief and rage he wiped out the entire Tusken Raider clan, including the children. He had let his feelings overpower him and had given in to his fear and anger. His journey to the dark side had begun.

Just as Palpatine is about to fall, Anakin lunges forward and cuts off Mace's lightsaber hand! As Mace stares at Anakin in shock, the Sith Lord springs to life, bombarding the Jedi Master with powerful

bolts of lightning. Unable to deflect the blasts with just one hand, Mace is flung out of the window and falls to his death. Palpatine cackles with delight. His face has changed into a terrible mask of evil.

Anakin is horrified. But Palpatine encourages the young Jedi to fulfil his destiny and become his apprentice – to learn to use the dark side of the Force. Anakin pauses, considering the terrible choice before him.

"Just help me save Padmé's life," he says at last. "I can't live without her. I want the power to stop death." He kneels before Palpatine. "I pledge myself to your teachings. To the ways of the Sith."

"Good, good," says Palpatine. "The Force is strong with you. Henceforth you shall be known as Darth Vader."

Believing the Jedi will come after Palpatine and Vader once they learn what they have done, the Sith Lord declares that every single one of them, including Obi-Wan Kenobi, is now an enemy of the

Republic. Palpatine sends Anakin to the Jedi Temple to destroy all the Jedi there, telling his new apprentice to show no mercy. Then he must go to the Mustafar system and wipe out Nute Gunray and the

The first to receive the order is Commander Cody on Utapau. Obi-Wan is able to avoid his attackers and jumps into the water at the bottom of a sinkhole.

On Kashyyyk, Commander Gree receives the order and moves to strike down Yoda. However, the elder Jedi Master is able to drop his assailants before they can get a shot off. Yoda and his two Wookiee protectors, Chewbacca and Tarfful, fight off a group of attacking clones before making an escape.

other Separatist leaders. At last the Sith will rule.

Now that Palpatine has transformed fully into Darth Sidious, he begins to contact clone commanders on all battlefronts to carry out Order 66: kill all Jedi.

But across the galaxy, other Jedi are not so lucky. Ki-Adi-Mundi is struck down on Mygeeto, Aayla Secura and Barriss Offee meet their deaths on Felucia, Plo Koon is shot down in the skies over Cato Neimoidia and Stass Allie is cut down on Saleucami.

News spreads that the Temple is under attack. Senator Bail Organa races aboard a speeder and sets down on a landing platform next to the Temple, where he is stopped by four troopers standing guard. Shots suddenly ring out, and Organa turns to see a Jedi youngling get struck down. A clone commander points at Organa.

"Get him! Shoot him!"

Several clones start firing as Organa jumps for cover behind his speeder. He starts it and clings to the side as it takes off and escapes.

After evading Cody's blaster fire and making his way through a series of caves, Obi-Wan returns to Grievous's secret landing platform. He boards a starfighter and

disappears into the sky. At the same time on Kashyyyk, Yoda boards a small escape pod and rockets away from the besieged world. The two remaining Jedi then meet Bail Organa aboard the Tantive IV to decide their next course of action.

During the pre-dawn hours on Coruscant, Padmé and C-3P0 watch the smoke rise from the Jedi Temple. Anakin and R2-D2 arrive. Anakin tells Padmé that

the Jedi tried to overthrow the Republic, explaining that Mace attempted to assassinate the Chancellor. Padmé can't understand how any of this could have happened. But Anakin insists that the Republic is unstable, and that the Jedi and a number of senators are traitors.

"I will not betray the Republic," says Anakin. "My loyalties lie with the Chancellor and with the Senate… and with you."

He tells her that she needs to distance herself from her friends in the Senate, and that the Chancellor will deal with them when the conflict is over.

"What about Obi-Wan?" she asks.

"I don't know," says Anakin. "Many Jedi have been killed."

Padmé fears she will be a suspect if an inquisition is started and wishes desperately to leave. Anakin assures her that he won't let anything happen to her and that they need to be here on Coruscant.

Anakin asks Padmé to have faith in him, and tells her that he has been given a special mission by the Chancellor to go to Mustafar; the Separatists have gathered there and it is up to him to set everything right and end the war.

"Please, wait for me," he says.

"I will," replies Padmé.

Aboard the *Tantive IV*, Bail Organa, Obi-Wan and Yoda discuss the past day's tragic events. None of them know what

happened or if any of the other Jedi are alive. Yoda explains that they have received a coded retreat message that tells all the Jedi to return to the Temple

because the war is over.

"We must go back!" exclaims Obi-Wan.

"If there are other stragglers, they will fall into the trap and be killed."

"Suggest dismantling the coded signal, do you?" asks Yoda. "I agree."

As the cruiser heads toward Coruscant,

it receives a message from the Chancellor's office. Mas Amedda appears on screen stating that the Supreme

Chancellor of the Republic requests Senator Organa's presence at a special session of Congress, to which he agrees. While Organa goes to the special session,

Yoda and Obi-Wan head for the Jedi Temple.

When they arrive at the Jedi Temple, Obi-Wan and Yoda eliminate a dozen clone troopers and make their way through the halls to dismantle the coded signal. As they hurry on, they discover many bodies of young students.

"Not even the younglings survived," says Obi-Wan, looking at the body of a young Padawan.

"Killed not by clones, this Padawan," says Yoda. "By a lightsaber, he was."

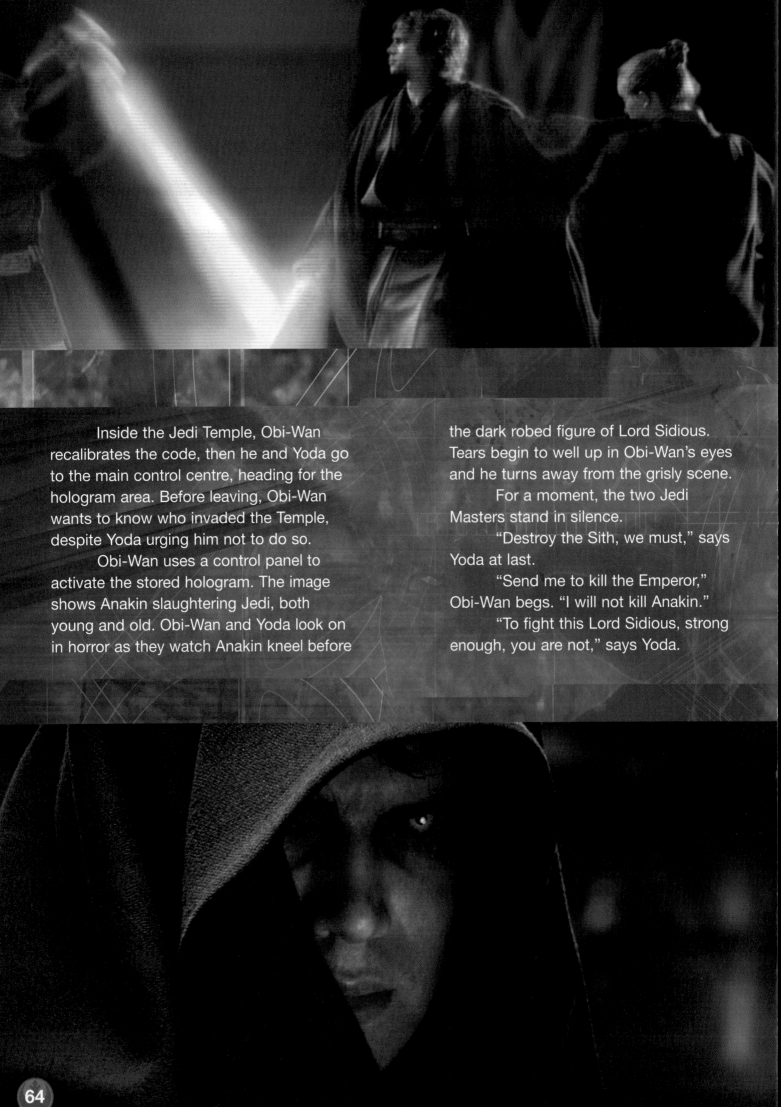

Inside the Jedi Temple, Obi-Wan recalibrates the code, then he and Yoda go to the main control centre, heading for the hologram area. Before leaving, Obi-Wan wants to know who invaded the Temple, despite Yoda urging him not to do so.

Obi-Wan uses a control panel to activate the stored hologram. The image shows Anakin slaughtering Jedi, both young and old. Obi-Wan and Yoda look on in horror as they watch Anakin kneel before the dark robed figure of Lord Sidious. Tears begin to well up in Obi-Wan's eyes and he turns away from the grisly scene.

For a moment, the two Jedi Masters stand in silence.

"Destroy the Sith, we must," says Yoda at last.

"Send me to kill the Emperor," Obi-Wan begs. "I will not kill Anakin."

"To fight this Lord Sidious, strong enough, you are not," says Yoda.

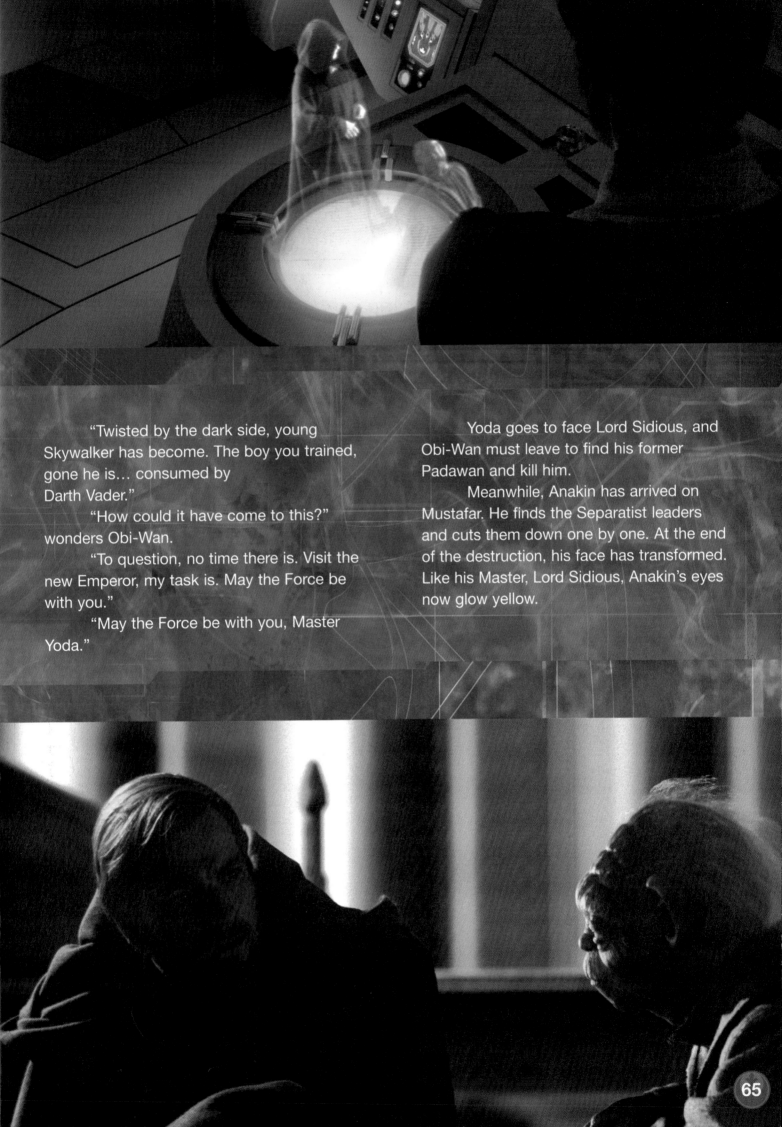

"Twisted by the dark side, young Skywalker has become. The boy you trained, gone he is... consumed by Darth Vader."

"How could it have come to this?" wonders Obi-Wan.

"To question, no time there is. Visit the new Emperor, my task is. May the Force be with you."

"May the Force be with you, Master Yoda."

Yoda goes to face Lord Sidious, and Obi-Wan must leave to find his former Padawan and kill him.

Meanwhile, Anakin has arrived on Mustafar. He finds the Separatist leaders and cuts them down one by one. At the end of the destruction, his face has transformed. Like his Master, Lord Sidious, Anakin's eyes now glow yellow.

In the Senate Building, Palpatine is addressing the crowd. Bail Organa takes a seat next to Padmé in the Naboo pod. She explains that the Chancellor has been telling them about the plot by the Jedi to overthrow the Senate. Bail knows the truth, but understands that nothing can be done about it at the present time. Palpatine says that all remaining Jedi will be hunted down and destroyed, and anyone who helped them will suffer the same fate. The Chancellor adds that the recent attempt on his life has left him scarred and deformed, but assures everyone that his resolve has never been stronger. After a long period of applause, Palpatine states that the Republic will be reorganised into the first Galactic Empire, for a safe and secure society that he says will last for ten thousand years. The Empire will be controlled by a sovereign ruler, who will be chosen for life, and a new constitution will be formed. Padmé is devastated.

"So this is how liberty dies," she says. "With thunderous applause…"

Later, Obi-Wan arrives at Padmé's apartment, where they tell each other the news: the Republic has fallen and the Jedi order is no more. Padmé has hope because the Senate is still intact, but Obi-Wan explains that the Sith now rule the galaxy. Obi-Wan asks Padmé if she knows where Anakin is, but she refuses to tell him.

"Padmé, Anakin has turned to the dark side," says Obi-Wan.

"You're wrong!" cries Padmé. "How can you even say that?"

Obi-Wan tells Padmé that Anakin killed the younglings, and that he has become Palpatine's apprentice, but she can't believe it.

Obi-Wan guesses that Anakin is the father of her child. He feels very sorry for her and for what he knows he must do. After Obi-Wan leaves, Padmé heads to a landing platform accompanied by C-3PO. Worried and tormented, she prepares to leave Coruscant and go to Mustafar to find Anakin. But before her Naboo skiff departs, Obi-Wan secretly boards the ship.

A hologram of Anakin appears in front of Sidious. He tells the Sith Lord that the Separatists are taken care of. Sidious praises his apprentice for a job well done, and then tells him to send a message to the ships of the Trade Federation, stating that the Separatist leaders, General Grievous and Count Dooku have been wiped out, and that all droid units are to be shut down immediately. As Anakin finishes his transmission, he sees Padmé's ship arriving and leaves to greet her.

Anakin runs to the ship and embraces Padmé. He asks what she's doing

Padmé desperately tries to stop Anakin, but it is too late. At last she realises her husband has changed.

"I don't know you any more. Anakin, you're breaking my heart. I'll never stop loving you, but you are going down a path I can't follow. Stop now. Come back! I love you."

But Anakin sees Obi-Wan in the doorway of the skiff and thinks Padmé has betrayed him.

"Liar!" he yells. "You brought him here to kill me!"

Anakin reaches out, grabs Padmé by

on Mustafar.

"I was so worried about you," she says. "Obi-Wan told me you have turned to the dark side."

Anakin becomes angry at the mention of his former Master's name.

"Obi-Wan is trying to turn you against me!" he says.

"Anakin, all I want is your love."

the throat and begins choking her.

Obi-Wan begs Anakin to let her go, and at last he releases his grip. Padmé crumples to the ground.

"You turned her against me," snarls Anakin.

"You have done that yourself," Obi-Wan replies. Both men throw off their cloaks and circle each other.

"You have become the very thing you swore to destroy," says Obi-Wan.

"If you're not with me, you're my enemy," Anakin replies.

They ignite their lightsabers and fight their way off the landing platform and into the main hallway.

Master Yoda enters the Chancellor's holding office. He uses the Force to throw two Royal Guards against a nearby wall, knocking them unconscious. Darth Sidious turns his chair toward Yoda. He raises his arms and shoots lightning bolts at the Jedi Master, engulfing him. Yoda is picked up by the blast and thrown across the room, where he hits the wall and slides down in a crumpled heap.

Sidious chuckles and approaches Yoda.

"I have waited a long time for this moment, my little green friend. At last, the Jedi are no more."

The Jedi uses the Force to throw the Sith Lord back, knocking him clear over his desk.

"At an end your rule is," says Yoda. Sidious picks himself up and flies through the air, heading towards the exit. At the last second, Yoda flies into the exit to stop him. Both ignite their lightsabers and clash in a fast and furious duel.

The fight moves into the Senate Chamber, where Sidious drops his lightsaber and shoots another barrage of lightning at Yoda. The Jedi Master deflects it back towards him. Sidious begins to hurl pod after pod at Yoda, who has to constantly duck and jump out of harm's way. The Jedi Master uses the Force to catch a pod in mid air and hurl it

back at Sidious, who leaps out of the way at the last instant.

As Yoda jumps after the fleeing Sith Lord, Sidious quickly turns and blasts the Jedi in mid air with a powerful volley of lightning, catching Yoda and throwing him back hard against the podium. The force of the blow causes the Jedi Master to drop his lightsaber, but he is still able to able to block the deadly bolts and throw Sidious off the podium. Yoda is also knocked down, and falls several hundred feet to the podium's base.

After his battle with Yoda, Sidious summons several clone troopers to search for the Jedi Master's body, but they find nothing. Sidious demands that they keep searching, then tells Mas Amedda to have his shuttle prepared for immediate takeoff - he senses Lord Vader is in danger.

Meanwhile, Yoda has made his way outside the Senate Building, where he awaits Bail Organa. As the senator's airspeeder slows and moves closer to a long row of lights, Yoda suddenly appears and falls out of one of the recesses into the speeder. Organa guns the engines and heads away from the building as fast as possible into the city traffic.

"Into exile I must go," says Yoda. "Failed, have I."

Anakin and Obi-Wan continue battling through Mustafar's main control centre and conference room and out onto the balcony.

Anakin begins using the Force to rip objects off the wall and hurl them at Obi-Wan, pushing him further and further along the walkway. The balcony ends, trapping Obi-Wan as he looks over the edge at the river of lava below. Anakin cuts a portion of railing off, along with a control panel. As alarms sound, a protective ray shield around the superstructure disappears and tumbles into the molten abyss. Obi-Wan has no choice but to tightrope-walk out across the lava river. They continue to fight as they reach the main collection plant. Anakin and Obi-Wan jump from one multi-spired panel to another. As the fighting intensifies, Obi-Wan is trapped. He grabs a cable and leaps from his position with Anakin in tow – the two Jedi continue fighting as they swing past each other. On the landing platform, C-3PO carries Padmé into the Naboo skiff.

The river drops off into a tremendous lava fall, causing Obi-Wan and Anakin to stop fighting. As the main part of the collector starts to break away and move towards the fall, Obi-Wan does a double back flip to land squarely on a floating platform. Anakin makes a running leap to

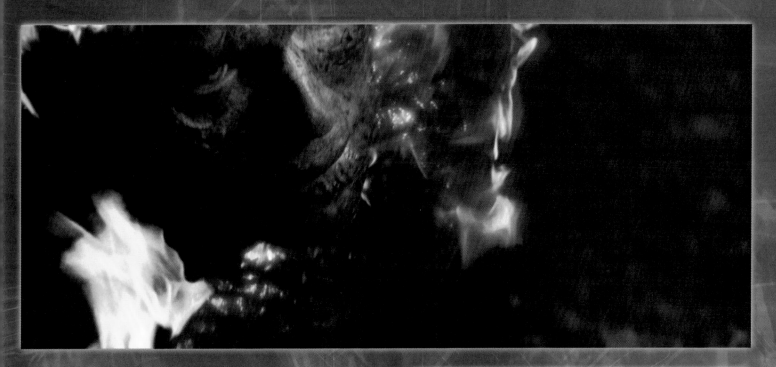

land on a worker droid, which he uses to catch up to Obi-Wan. With both men on the platform, the fighting continues until Obi-Wan jumps towards the safety of the black sandy edge of the river, gaining the high ground.

"I have failed you, Anakin," says Obi-Wan.

"This is the end for you, my Master," says Anakin.

"Don't try it," warns Obi-Wan.

As Anakin attempts to follow his former Master, Obi-Wan cuts his young apprentice at the knees, and then cuts off his left arm in the blink of an eye. Anakin tumbles down the embankment, rolling to a stop near the edge of the lava. Obi-Wan picks up Anakin's lightsaber and looks back.

"I hate you!" Anakin cries.

"You were my brother, Anakin," says Obi-Wan. "I loved you."

Anakin's clothing blows into the lava and ignites. Anakin becomes engulfed in flames and starts screaming, struggling to crawl back up the embankment. Obi-Wan runs back to Padmé's ship as Anakin drops, smouldering, near the top of the lava pit. As Obi-Wan walks over to where Padmé is lying, she asks Obi-Wan if Anakin is all right. He looks at her sadly, but does not answer.

He brushes her hair back as she slips back into unconsciousness.

Not long after Anakin is left to die, Darth Sidious's shuttle lands on Mustafar. A platoon of clone troopers exits the craft, followed by the Dark Lord.

"Anakin!" cries Darth Sidious. "There he is! He's still alive."

The clones prepare a medical capsule. Once they have Vader secured in the belly of the craft, the ship quickly takes off.

On the isolated asteroid of Polis Massa, Yoda begins to meditate and hears the voice of Qui-Gon Jinn. Qui-Gon tells Yoda that it is possible to become one with the Force. It is possible to defy death, but only for oneself, and Darth Plagueis never managed it. The state can only be acquired through compassion, not greed. Therefore a Sith Lord can never achieve this form of higher consciousness. Yoda gratefully agrees to become Qui-Gon's apprentice and learn how to become one with the Force.

As Yoda finishes his meditation, Bail Organa tells him Obi-Wan has made

contact. They go to the landing platform where Kenobi lands the Naboo cruiser. Obi-Wan, followed by R2-D2 and C-3PO,

emerges from the ramp carrying the unconscious Padmé in his arms. She is quickly taken to the asteroid's medical

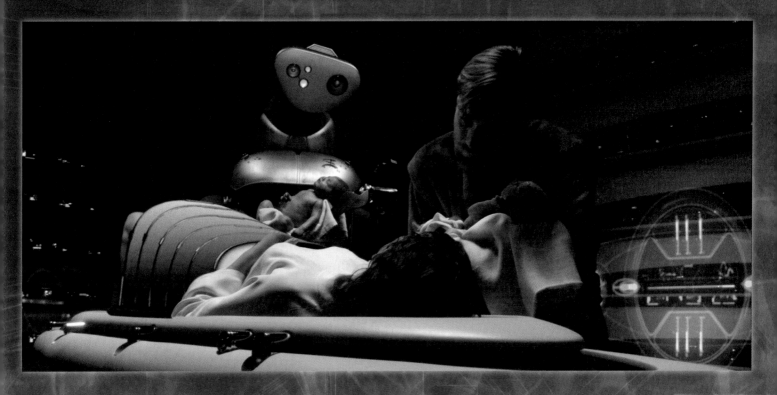

centre.

The Polis Massa medics work on Padmé in the operating room.

"Medically, she is completely healthy," a medical droid explains. "For reasons we cannot explain, we are losing her. She has lost the will to live."

"She's dying?" asks Obi-Wan.

"We need to operate quickly if we are to save the babies," continues the droid. "She's carrying twins."

"Save them, we must," says Yoda. "They are our last hope."

Obi-Wan is with Padmé as she gives birth, first to a boy called Luke and then to a girl called Leia. Obi-Wan leans over Padmé.

"Don't give up," he urges her. But Padmé can only give a faint smile.

"Obi-Wan, there is still good in him,"

she whispers, wincing in pain. "There… is… still…"

With a last gasp of pain, Padmé dies. Obi-Wan is left holding her hand.

On Coruscant, Anakin's near-lifeless body is carried along in the floating medical capsule to the Imperial Rehabilitation Centre. Once there, Anakin is lifted onto a table where droids go to work on him, giving him brand new legs and a new arm.

Darth Sidious hovers around the droids as they work on Anakin. At last nose plugs are inserted and a terrible mask drops from above, sealing tightly. The helmet is fitted and Vader begins breathing.

The table where Darth Vader lies begins to rise and Sidious moves up to it. Darth Vader is encased in a hard black suit, as menacing as his helmet.

"Lord Vader, can you hear me?" asks Sidious.

"Yes, my Master," replies Vader. He looks at Sidious. "Where is Padmé? Is she safe, is she all right?"

"It seems in your anger, you killed her," Sidious replies.

A low groan comes from Vader's mask.

"I couldn't have! She was alive! I felt it."

Suddenly everything in the room begins to implode, including some of the droids. Darth Sidious gives an evil smile as Vader's screams of agony echo throughout the Centre.

Aboard the Alderaan cruiser, Bail Organa, Yoda, and Obi-Wan are making plans to send Padmé's body back to Naboo. She still needs to appear pregnant, because the children must be hidden and kept somewhere safe where the Sith will never sense their presence. It is decided that the children should be split up.

"My wife and I will take the girl," says Organa. "She will be loved with us."

"And what of the boy?" asks Obi-Wan.

"To Tatooine," says Yoda. "To his family, send him."

"I will take the child and watch over him," says Obi-Wan. "Do you think Anakin's twins will be able to defeat Lord Sidious?"

"Strong the Force runs, in the Skywalker line," says Yoda. "Hope, we can."

After Bail leaves the conference room, Yoda tells Obi-Wan that he will teach him how to commune with his long-departed Master, Qui-Gon Jinn. On Tatooine Qui-Gon will teach him how to become one with

the Force.

And so, across the galaxy, the preparations begin...

On the planet of Naboo, a large crowd gathers to pay their final respects to Padmé as she is laid to rest.

Across the galaxy, a small pod hurls its way towards the planet Dagobah. When it lands, Yoda's tiny form emerges to survey the unfamiliar terrain.

From the bridge of a Star Destroyer, the Emperor, Governor Grand Moff Tarkin and Darth Vader watch as the huge frame of the Death Star begins to take shape.

On the planet of Alderaan, Bail Organa gives Leia to his wife.

And on Tatooine, Obi-Wan arrives at the home of Owen and Beru Lars. He hands baby Luke to them. As Obi-Wan leaves, the family stands near the ridge of the homestead and watches the twin suns set.

JOURNEY TO THE DARK SIDE

Shmi Skywalker

Anakin Skywalker m. Padmé Amidala

Luke

Leia

After struggling with his feelings, Anakin married Padmé in a secret ceremony, disobeying his Jedi vows as the Clone Wars began. Neither of them could guess what terrible consequences their marriage would have. Palpatine sensed Anakin's feelings of fear, loss and anger, and was determined to use them to destroy the Republic and become Emperor.

When Anakin started to have nightmare visions of Padmé dying, Palpatine told him about a Sith Lord who had learned how to stop death. Anakin loved Padmé above everything, even his Jedi vows. He was determined to find a way to save her life.

Anakin was torn between his Jedi vows and his fears for Padmé. Sensing a void in the youth's spirit, Senator Palpatine offered him a quicker path to power – that of the dark side. Anakin struggled with his feelings, but at last, filled with suspicion and doubt, he put his trust in Palpatine and turned his back on the Jedi order.

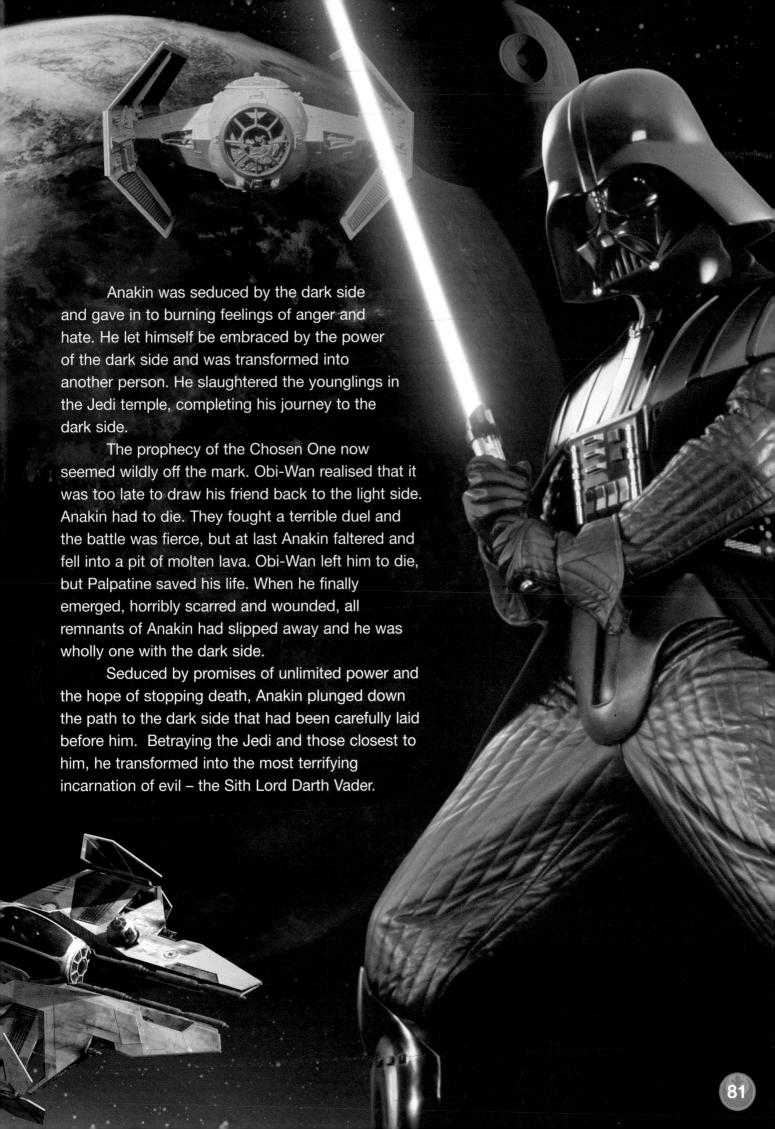

Anakin was seduced by the dark side and gave in to burning feelings of anger and hate. He let himself be embraced by the power of the dark side and was transformed into another person. He slaughtered the younglings in the Jedi temple, completing his journey to the dark side.

The prophecy of the Chosen One now seemed wildly off the mark. Obi-Wan realised that it was too late to draw his friend back to the light side. Anakin had to die. They fought a terrible duel and the battle was fierce, but at last Anakin faltered and fell into a pit of molten lava. Obi-Wan left him to die, but Palpatine saved his life. When he finally emerged, horribly scarred and wounded, all remnants of Anakin had slipped away and he was wholly one with the dark side.

Seduced by promises of unlimited power and the hope of stopping death, Anakin plunged down the path to the dark side that had been carefully laid before him. Betraying the Jedi and those closest to him, he transformed into the most terrifying incarnation of evil – the Sith Lord Darth Vader.

YODA
Jedi Trials

You have reached the next stage of your training and you are doing well. But more difficult your tasks will now become.

1

Jedi are not allowed to have any emotional attachments. But you have fallen in love. What do you do?

a. Ignore your feelings and hope they will go away.
b. Give in to your feelings and lie to the Jedi Council.
c. Accept that you cannot always follow your heart. Use your feelings to become a better Jedi.

2

During battle your friend is hit by a blaster. What do you do?

a. Forget about the battle and go to help your friend.
b. You are worried for your friend, but you carry on fighting. It is your Jedi duty to defeat this enemy.
c. Leave your friend and attack your enemy, keen to get revenge.

3

Your Jedi Master is teaching you to levitate objects with the power of concentration. Suddenly your astromech droid starts beeping urgently. What do you do?

a. Try to ignore the droid.
b. Run to find out what the problem is – you can continue your training later.
c. Try to understand what the droid is saying without losing concentration.

4

A great Jedi tells you that you will become even more powerful than Master Yoda. How does this make you feel?

a. Concerned – a Jedi should not think of personal glory.
b. Flattered and excited about the future.
c. Doubtful – you know you can never be that powerful.

5

Your Jedi Master tells you to do something that seems impossible. What do you do?

a. Try to do it feeling angry – does he want to make you look stupid?
b. You do it of course – your Master is wise and knows what a Jedi is capable of doing.
c. Tell your Master that he is asking the impossible.

6

The Jedi Council tells you that you are not yet ready to take the trials to become a Jedi Knight. How do you feel?

a. A bit relieved – you knew you weren't ready.
b. You accept the decision, knowing that your time will come.
c. Frustrated – you are so keen to show how talented you are!

Count up your scores and add them to your previous totals. There are more tests to come before you reach the level of Jedi Knight.

①
a. 2
b. 6
c. 10

②
a. 2
b. 10
c. 6

③
a. 6
b. 2
c. 10

④
a. 10
b. 6
c. 2

⑤
a. 6
b. 10
c. 2

⑥
a. 2
b. 10
c. 6

JEDI ARCHIVE

LANDO CALRISSIAN

Lando Calrissian is a gambler who became Cloud City's Baron Administrator after winning the title in a game of sabacc. He has the spirit of a soldier-of-fortune and the heart of a high-stakes player. Lando owned Han Solo's ship, the *Millennium Falcon*, for years before he lost it to Han in a game of sabacc.

HAN SOLO

This smuggler is willing to take huge risks for tremendous gains. Charming and impulsive, he has a wide lucky streak and a great deal of arrogance. The Wookiee Chewbacca is his constant companion and confidante. Han runs a regular glitterstim-spice smuggling route for the likes of Jabba the Hutt.

CHEWBACCA

The Wookiee Chewbacca is very loyal and as strong as a gladiator. He has seen life as a slave, a smuggler and a top-notch pilot and mechanic, and was rescued from his slave ship by Han Solo. He now accompanies Han on his smuggling missions across the galaxy.

JABBA THE HUTT

Jabba the Hutt rules a vast criminal empire from his desert palace on Tatooine. He is an unforgiving and sadistic crime lord. Thieves, smugglers, assassins, spies and all manner of criminals are constantly at his side and he is involved in every kind of illegal enterprise throughout the Outer Rim.

EMPEROR PALPATINE

Palpatine is a diabolical Dark Jedi who rules the galaxy through fear. He encourages hatred, racism and tyranny. He used Darth Vader to hound the Jedi Knights, slaughtering them to ensure that he would never be challenged. Palpatine has ordered the building of incredibly destructive starships, space stations and weapons.

IDENTITY FILES

YODA

Short in height but great in the Force, this long-lived Jedi Master trained Jedi Knights in the ways of the Force for 800 years. When Emperor Palpatine ordered his purge of the Jedi, Yoda went into hiding. He used the Force to discourage visitors and to keep a watch on Luke Skywalker and Leia Organa.

OBI-WAN KENOBI

After Anakin Skywalker turned to the dark side, Obi-Wan Kenobi helped to hide his twin son and daughter. Living as a reclusive old hermit by the Western Dune Sea on Tatooine, the once great Jedi Knight kept track of young Luke Skywalker as the Empire sought out and destroyed most of the galaxy's remaining Jedi Knights.

LUKE SKYWALKER

The son of Padmé and Anakin, Luke is strong in the Force. He always accepts the greatest challenges and also challenges others to do their best. Raised on Tatooine by his aunt and uncle, he had no idea of his true history until destiny brought the fate of the entire galaxy to his doorstep.

LEIA ORGANA

Leia was taken by Senator Bail Organa of Alderan to be raised as his daughter. The young princess grew up enmeshed in the politics of her time. She has a deep commitment to peace, freedom and democracy and became the youngest Senator in galactic history.

C-3PO

C-3PO is a golden protocol droid who makes up half of the most famous robot team in the galaxy. Along with his squat companion R2-D2, C-3PO has had enough adventures to fill several lives since first being activated.

SHIPS AND MACHINES

MILLENNIUM FALCON

DESCRIPTION:	MODIFIED YT-1300 TRANSPORT
SIZE:	26.7M LONG
SPEED:	1,050KPH
WEAPONS:	2 QUAD LASER CANNONS, 2 CONCUSSION MISSILE TUBES, BLASTER CANNON
CREW/ PASSENGERS:	2 CREW + 6 PASSENGERS

DEATH STAR

DESCRIPTION:	A BATTLE STATION WITH A SUPERLASER DESIGNED TO DESTROY PLANETS
SIZE:	120KM DIAMETER
SPEED:	CLASS 4 HYPERDRIVE
WEAPONS:	1 SUPERLASER, 5,000 TURBOLASER BATTERIES, 5,000 HEAVY TURBOLASERS, 2,500 LASER CANNONS, 2,500 ION CANNONS, 768 TRACTOR-BEAM EMPLACEMENTS AND OVER 11,000 COMBAT VEHICLES
CREW/ PASSENGERS:	265,675 CREW, 57,276 GUNNERS + 843,342 PASSENGERS

THETA-CLASS SHUTTLE

DESCRIPTION:	IMPERIAL-CLASS LANDING SHUTTLE DESIGNED TO DEPLOY TROOPS
SIZE:	18.5M LONG
SPEED:	2,000KPH
WEAPONS:	9 LASER CANONS
CREW/ PASSENGERS:	5 CREW + 20 PASSENGERS (DEPENDINDING ON CONFIGURATION)

IMPERIAL STAR DESTROYER

DESCRIPTION:	IMPERIAL I-CLASS MAMMOTH STARSHIP DESIGNED FOR PURSUIT-AND-CAPTURE OPERATIONS
SIZE:	1,600M LONG
SPEED:	2,300G
WEAPONS:	60 TURBOLASER BATTERIES, 60 ION CANNONS, 10 TRACTOR BEAM PROJECTORS
CREW/ PASSENGERS:	9,235 OFFICERS, 27,850 ENLISTED, CARRIES 9,700 TROOPS, 72 TIE FIGHTERS, 15 STORMTROOPER TRANSPORTS, 20 AT-AT WALKERS, 30 AT-ST SCOUT WALKERS

TIE ADVANCED FIGHTER

DESCRIPTION: DARTH VADER'S FIGHTER, USED AT THE BATTLE OF YAVIN

SIZE: 9.2M LONG

SPEED: 1,200KPH

WEAPONS: 2 LASER CANNONS

CREW/ PASSENGERS: 1 PILOT

EXECUTOR

DESCRIPTION: DARTH VADER'S COMMAND SHIP

SIZE: 19,000M LONG

SPEED: 1,230G

WEAPONS: 250 TURBOLASER BATTERIES, 250 HEAVY TURBOLASER BATTERIES, 250 CONCUSSION MISSILE TUBES, 250 ION CANNONS, 40 TRACTOR BEAM PROJECTORS

CREW/ PASSENGERS: CREW: 280,735, CARRIES 38,000 STORMTROOPERS, 144 TIE FIGHTERS, 200 COMBAT AND SUPPORT VEHICLES

AT-AT WALKER

DESCRIPTION: IMPERIAL ALL TERRAIN TRANSPORT USED FOR GROUND ASSAULTS

SIZE: 20.6M LONG

SPEED: 60KPH

WEAPONS: 2 HEAVY LASER CANNONS, 3 MEDIUM BLASTERS

CREW/ PASSENGERS: 3 CREW, CARRIES 40 STORMTROOPERS, 5 SPEEDER BIKES

AT-ST WALKER

DESCRIPTION: IMPERIAL ALL TERRAIN SCOUT TRANSPORT GROUND SUPPORT VEHICLE

SIZE: 8.6M TALL

SPEED: 90KPH

WEAPONS: 1 TWIN BLASTER CANNON, 1 TWIN LIGHT BLASTER CANNON, CONCUSSION GRENADE LAUNCHER

CREW/ PASSENGERS: 2 CREW

IMPERIAL SPEEDER BIKE

DESCRIPTION: PERSONAL TRANSPORT FOR SCOUT TROOPS ON RECONNAISSANCE

SIZE: 4.4M LONG

SPEED: 500 KPH

WEAPONS: 1 LIGHT BLASTER CANNON

CREW/ PASSENGERS: 1 PILOT

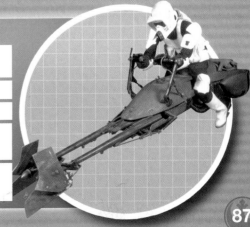

Helmet contains body heat regulators, air pump, electrical system radiators, air processing filter, primary environmental sensor, nutrient feed tube and voice processor

DARTH VADER

Anakin Skywalker turned his back on all that he once held dear when he became the evil Sith apprentice Darth Vader. He betrayed his fellow Jedi, his friends and even his beloved Padmé. The personification of the evil and fear that Emperor Palpatine uses to rule the galaxy, Vader helped hunt down and exterminate nearly all the remaining Jedi Knights. He commands by terror and is more machine than man. Vader obeys the Emperor's every command and destroys all who stand in his way.

Vocoder

Durasteel armour

Life system computer control

Respiratory sensor matrix

Temperature regulation system

Internal comlink

Helmet contains
advanced sensors

Macrobinocular
view plate

Grenade launcher

Jetpack

Wrist blasters

Miniature flame thrower

Kneepad rocket dart
launchers

Spiked boots

BOBA FETT

The unaltered clone of Jango Fett, Boba has grown up to be a merciless bounty hunter. Hired by the gangster Jabba the Hutt, he has pursued Han Solo and Chewbacca across the galaxy. His fearsome Mandalorian armour makes him a walking arsenal and he is one of the Rebellion's most persistent opponents.

Domed head contains infrared receptors, electromagnetic-field sensors, a register readout and logic dispenser, dedicated energy receptors, a radar eye, heat and motion detectors and a holographic recorder and projector

Spacecraft linkage
and repair arms

Treaded legs provide mobility and a
third leg can drop down for extra
stability on rough terrain

R2-D2

R2-D2 is a loyal, inventive and sarcastic astromech droid. He has developed an odd relationship with C-3PO over the years and they have deep mutual respect and trust for each other. Behind doors in his cylindrical body lie hidden instruments, including a storage/retrieval jack for computer linkup, auditory receivers, flame-retardant foam dispenser, electric shock prod, high-powered spotlight, grasping claw, laser welder, circular saw and a cybot acoustic signaller.

EPISODE 4
A NEW HOPE

It is a period of civil war. Rebel spaceships, striking from a hidden base, have won their first victory against the evil Galactic Empire.

During the battle, Rebel spies managed to steal secret plans of the Empire's ultimate weapon, the Death Star, an armoured space station with enough power to destroy an entire planet.

Pursued by the Empire's sinister agent, Darth Vader, Princess Leia races home aboard her starship, with the stolen plans that can restore freedom to the galaxy.

The Imperial ship is too fast for them, and soon catches them up. Darth Vader stalks through the ship over the dead bodies of the princess's guards. The princess gives the plans to R2-D2 just before she is captured.

R2-D2 escapes in an escape pod with C-3P0, and Darth Vader sends a detachment after them to retrieve them.

R2-D2 and C-3P0 land on the nearby planet of Tatooine, in the middle of a vast desert. But they are captured by Sand People, who steal robots and sell them on. They are taken to a small moisture farm, where they are bought by Owen Lars.

Owen tells his nephew, Luke Skywalker, to clean his new droids up and set them to work. But while Luke is cleaning R2-D2, he dislodges part of the hidden message from the princess to Obi-Wan Kenobi, begging him for help.

Luke longs for adventure and does not really want to stay on the farm with his uncle. But his uncle does not want him to leave because he is afraid he has too much of his father in him. They have never told Luke the truth about his father. When he tells his aunt and uncle about the message for Obi-Wan, they are worried.

While they are at dinner, R2-D2 goes off in search of Obi-Wan Kenobi, who lives on the other side of the Dune Sea.

Next morning, Luke and C-3P0 follow R2-D2. They find him and they also find Obi-Wan Kenobi, who tells Luke that his father was a Jedi Knight and a great star pilot. Luke learns that his father, Anakin Skywalker, was killed by Darth Vader, who was once Obi-Wan's Padawan pupil. Obi-Wan gives Luke his father's lightsaber and tells him about the Force. Darth Vader has now turned to the dark side of the Force.

R2-D2 plays the message from the princess. She begs Obi-Wan to take the plans of the Death Star to her father on Alderaan. Obi-Wan asks Luke to join him and go to Alderaan with him. But Luke refuses because of his duty to his uncle.

However, when they return to the Lars homestead, they find it has been torched by Vader's search detachment. Luke's aunt and uncle are dead.

Luke decides to join Obi-Wan on his mission to Alderaan. He wants to learn the ways of the Force and become a Jedi Knight, like his father.

The travellers arrive at Mos Eisley spaceport, where Obi-Wan hopes to find a ship to take them to Alderaan. They hire a pilot called Han Solo and his Wookiee first mate, Chewbacca, who have a fast ship called the *Millennium Falcon*.

On the Death Star, Princess Leia is tortured by Darth Vader but will not reveal the location of the Rebels' secret base. He sets their course for her home planet of Alderaan.

Han Solo owes money to a gangster on Tatooine called Jabba the Hutt. He promises to come back with the money after his trip to Alderaan. A bounty hunter called Boba Fett listens with interest.

Darth Vader's stormtroopers have discovered where they are, and they fire on the *Millennium Falcon* as it leaves Tatooine.

When the Death Star reaches Alderaan, Princess Leia is told to reveal the location of the Rebel base or her home planet will be destroyed. She tells them it is on Dantooine, but they blow up Alderaan anyway, killing all her people and her family.

Leia has lied about the location of the Rebel base, so she is placed in the detention cells to await execution.

Far away on the *Millennium Falcon*, Obi-Wan is beginning to instruct Luke in the ways of the Jedi when he feels a terrible disturbance in the Force. It has been caused by the destruction of Alderaan. They come out of light speed and see only the Death Star where Alderaan should be.

Darth Vader realises that this is the ship that escaped his stormtroopers on Tatooine and it must be carrying the stolen plans. The Death Star draws them in with a tractor beam. Han, Luke and Chewbacca overpower the guards and hide in the battle station.

Darth Vader senses Obi-Wan's presence and goes to search for his old Master. "I must face him alone," he says.

Han and Luke realise that they must deactivate the tractor beam that is holding them by causing a power loss at the main power terminals. Obi-Wan says he will do this. "The Force will be with you, always," he tells Luke as he leaves.

R2-D2 discovers that the princess is on board in a detention centre. Han, Luke and Chewbacca go to rescue her, but after releasing her they are trapped. Leia shoots a hole in the garbage chute and makes an escape route for them. They all jump in and get away from the stormtroopers who are firing on them. "Wonderful girl!" shouts Han.

Obi-Wan finds the power terminal and shuts it down. The tractor beam holding the *Millennium Falcon* is deactivated. Luke, Leia, Han and Chewbacca fight their way past stormtroopers and make it back to the *Millennium Falcon*.

Meanwhile, Darth Vader has come face to face with Obi-Wan. They ignite their lightsabers.

"We meet again at last," says Darth Vader. "Now I am the master."

"Only a master of evil," replies Obi-Wan. "If you strike me down I shall become more powerful than you can possibly imagine."

After long years, they once more lock sabers in battle. But after a powerful duel, Obi-Wan holds up his lightsaber and closes his eyes, accepting his destiny at the hands of his old Padawan. Darth Vader strikes Obi-Wan down and his body vanishes.

Darth Vader allows the *Millennium Falcon* to escape, but commands the Death Star to follow it. The *Falcon* leads them to Yavin 4, the headquarters of the Rebellion.

With the plans that Princess Leia has brought them, the Rebels know that the Death Star has one weakness, but the target area is only two metres wide. A precise hit on the thermal exhaust port will destroy the entire battle station.

Luke is piloting a fighter, but Han decides to leave to pay off his debt to Jabba the Hutt. Luke and Leia are angry with him for going as the great battle begins. The Rebel pilots speed into space to engage the Imperial enemy.

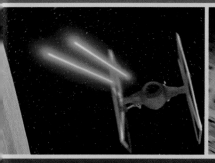

Darth Vader is piloting his own fighter. He is still a magnificent pilot and destroys many Rebel fighters.

The Rebel leaders try to hit the tiny target, but they fail. With only a minute left before the Death Star will be in range to destroy Yavin 4, Luke prepares to try. He is now the Rebels' only hope. But Darth Vader is on his tail.

Luke's computer tries to focus on the target. But Luke hears the voice of Obi-Wan Kenobi, telling him to use the Force. Luke switches off the computer and uses the Force to guide him instead.

"The Force is strong with this one!" exclaims Darth Vader. He is close behind Luke now, but suddenly the *Millennium Falcon* appears above him and blasts his fighter, sending him whirling into space. Han has not left them in their hour of need!

Luke sends his photon torpedoes straight into the target using the power of the Force. The Death Star explodes into millions of tiny burning pieces, but Darth Vader has escaped.

Cheered by the Rebel troops, Luke, Chewbacca and Han receive medals from Princess Leia. Together they have created new hope that the Empire can one day be destroyed.

EPISODE 5

THE EMPIRE STRIKES BACK

It is a dark time for the Rebellion. Although the Death Star has been destroyed, Imperial troops have driven the Rebel forces from their hidden base and pursued them across the galaxy.

Evading the dreaded Imperial Starfleet, a group of freedom fighters led by Luke Skywalker has established a new secret base on the remote ice world of Hoth.

The evil lord Darth Vader, obsessed with finding young Skywalker, has dispatched thousands of remote probes into the far reaches of space. One probe lands on Hoth.

Han and Luke have just finished a routine area check of the freezing ice world. Han returns to the base but Luke sees the probe and thinks it is a meteor. When he goes to check, a terrible snow beast attacks him and drags him away.

At the base, Han tells Leia that he has to leave to pay off Jabba the Hutt. By now Jabba has hired bounty hunters to track him down. Leia is angry with Han for leaving and they argue. But before Han can go, C-3P0 and R2-D2 report that Luke is missing. If he is not back before nightfall, he will die out in the snowy wastes of Hoth. So Han goes to search for his friend.

Luke wakes up in the beast's cave and uses his lightsaber to free himself. He escapes from the beast, but collapses in the freezing snow. Then he sees Obi-Wan Kenobi standing in front of him.

"Go to the Dagobah system," says Obi-Wan. "There you will learn from Yoda, the Jedi Master who instructed me."

As Obi-Wan fades away, Luke passes out. But Han finds him just in time and saves his life.

On board his starship, Darth Vader gets a transmission from his probe and sets a course for Hoth. Back at the base, the sensors detect the probe and intercept its transmission. They realise that the Empire knows where they are and they have to evacuate the base.

The Rebel forces agree on a rendezvous point and prepare to leave. But Darth Vader arrives before they have evacuated and sends troops down to the planet for a surface attack. There is a mighty battle between the Rebels and the Imperial stormtroopers as the Rebel forces are evacuated.

Luke helps fight the Imperial ground troops and risks his life to destroy their walkers. Then he escapes in his fighter ship with R2-D2, setting a course for the Dagobah system.

Han and Chewbacca escape just in time with Princess Leia and C-3P0. Darth Vader is furious to have missed them again. He orders his starship to chase them. Han discovers that the hyperdrive motivator has been damaged and it is impossible to go to lightspeed. He flies into an asteroid field and hides inside a crater on one of the asteroids.

Darth Vader summons some bounty hunters to capture the Millennium Falcon. One of them is Boba Fett.

Luke arrives on Dagobah and crash lands in a swamp. He sets up camp in a clearing and meets a small, comical creature with green skin and large ears. Luke explains that he is looking for a great warrior, and the little being promises to take him to Yoda.

Darth Vader reports to the Emperor, who tells him that Luke is the son of Anakin Skywalker. The Emperor orders that the son of Skywalker must not become a Jedi, because the Force is so strong with him that he could destroy them. But if they can turn him to the dark side, he will become a powerful ally.

On Dagobah, Luke grows impatient. He demands to be taken to Yoda at once. The strange being turns away and says,

"I cannot teach him; he is not ready." Luke hears Obi-Wan reply, and realises that this is Yoda. Together he and Obi-Wan persuade Yoda to train him.

"I won't fail you," says Luke. "I'm not afraid."

"You will be," Yoda replies.

Luke finds his training very tough. He learns that a Jedi's strength flows from the Force, but that anger, fear and aggression are the dark side of the Force. He must learn to stay calm and use the Force for knowledge and defence – never for attack. He has a lot to learn – can he overcome his fear and doubts?

Still hidden in the asteroid, Han cannot repair the *Millennium Falcon* because they need new parts. He decides to go to a nearby mining colony, which is run by his friend Lando Calrissian. There they will find the parts they need.

Darth Vader's Imperial ship detects the *Millennium Falcon* as it leaves the asteroid field. They fire on it, but suddenly it disappears from their radar. They think that it has gone into light speed, but Han is playing a trick on them. He has turned off all power and attached himself to the side of their ship.

When the Imperial ship jettisons its rubbish before going to light speed, Han floats away with it. Darth Vader's ship goes into hyperspace and the *Millennium Falcon* speeds off in the opposite direction. But Han

and Chewbacca do not know that the bounty hunter Boba Fett is following them.

Meanwhile, Luke is improving – he is learning to feel the Force and be calm. But then he has a vision of Han and Leia in danger in a city in the clouds. He says he must go to help them. Yoda tells him that he must not leave without completing his training – it is too dangerous. Obi-Wan also tries to persuade him. Only a fully trained Jedi Knight can conquer Darth Vader and the Emperor. But it is no use. Luke promises to return and complete his training, and takes off with R2-D2 to help his friends.

"That boy is our last hope," says Obi-Wan sadly.

"No," says Yoda. "There is another."

The *Millennium Falcon* lands at the mining colony. It is a city in the clouds. Han's friend Lando greets them, but Leia is suspicious of him. After a few days, Lando tricks them and delivers them to Darth Vader. Boba Fett told him their location and Lando was forced to make a deal. Chewbacca and Han are tortured and thrown into a cell with Leia and C-3P0.

Darth Vader knows that Luke will come to rescue his friends. He plans to put Luke in a carbon freezing facility and take him to the Emperor, but first he tests it on Han, who is frozen solid in carbonite. Darth Vader gives him to Boba Fett, who plans to take him to Jabba the Hutt and collect the reward.

When Luke arrives at the mining colony, he sees Lando leading Leia, C-3P0 and Chewbacca away with stormtroopers. Luke follows them into a hangar, but it's a trap. Luke turns and sees the glinting black figure of Darth Vader.

"The Force is strong with you, young Skywalker," he says. "But you are not a Jedi yet!"

They ignite their lightsabers and begin to duel.

Lando feels very guilty. He frees Leia and Chewbacca and they find R2-D2 and fight past stormtroopers to the *Millennium Falcon*. They take off just in time and speed away to safety.

Luke defends himself well, but Darth Vader is better. Finally Luke falls on a platform above a bottomless drop. Darth Vader swipes at him with his red lightsaber and cuts off his right hand! Luke's hand and his lightsaber fall over the edge of the platform and disappear. Then Darth Vader reveals his great secret.

"I am your father," he says.

Luke is horrified, but his feelings tell him it is true. Darth Vader says it is his destiny to turn to the dark side. He asks Luke to destroy the Emperor so they can rule the galaxy together as father and son. But Luke would rather die. He rolls over the edge of the platform and drops into the abyss.

Far below, Luke manages to break his fall by clinging to a metal structure below the city. Something makes him call for Leia. Far away, on the escaping *Millennium Falcon,* Leia hears him and tells Lando and Chewbacca to turn the ship around and rescue him. Darth Vader senses that Luke is still alive and tries to stop them, but they put the *Millennium Falcon* into hyperspace and escape with Luke at light speed.

At the Rebel rendezvous, Luke is given a false hand. Lando and Chewbacca prepare to go after Boba Fett and rescue Han from Jabba the Hutt.

Luke and Leia watch as the *Millennium Falcon* speeds away through the stars.

RETURN OF THE JEDI

Luke Skywalker has returned to his home planet of Tatooine to rescue his friend Han Solo from the clutches of the vile gangster Jabba the Hutt. Lando Calrissian and Chewbacca never returned from their rescue mission.

The Galactic Empire has secretly begun construction on a new Death Star. When completed, this ultimate weapon will spell certain doom for the Rebels struggling to restore freedom to the galaxy.

On the half-completed Death Star, Lord Vader's shuttle arrives in the landing bay. He tells the commander that the Emperor himself is coming to oversee the creation. He does not feel that work is moving fast enough.

On Tatooine, Luke carries out a daring plan to rescue Han from Jabba the Hutt. Leia, Chewbacca, Lando and the droids all help to save Han. Jabba tries to throw the friends into the pit of Carkoon, but he is defeated and killed, and Boba Fett is thrown into the pit instead.

Back on the *Millennium Falcon*, Leia and Han fly to meet the Alliance Rebels with Lando, Chewbacca and C-3P0. But Luke and R2-D2 set a course for the Dagobah system. Luke has a promise to keep.

Meanwhile the Emperor's ship has landed on the Death Star. The black-cloaked Emperor greets Darth Vader and tells him that he must bring Luke to him. He has grown stronger, and only together can they now turn him to the dark side.

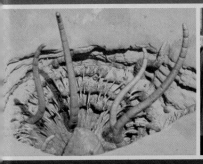

When Luke returns to the Dagobah system, he finds that Yoda is dying. Yoda tells Luke that he requires no more training, but he must confront Darth Vader before he can truly be a Jedi. He reminds Luke that a Jedi's strength flows from the Force. Then he dies and his body vanishes, just as Obi-Wan's did after his battle with Darth Vader.

As Luke grieves for Yoda, Obi-Wan appears next to him. He explains that Anakin was seduced by the dark side of the Force. He ceased to be Anakin Skywalker and became Darth Vader. Luke is overcome with pity for his father and believes that there is still good in him. He refuses to kill him.

"Then the Emperor has already won," says Obi-Wan sadly.

Obi-Wan also tells Luke that he has a twin sister, and Luke's insight tells him that his sister is Leia. He returns to rendezvous with the Rebel Alliance.

The Rebel Alliance is making its final plans to attack the Empire. To destroy the Death Star, they must deactivate its energy shield. The energy shield is powered from the forest moon of Endor. When they have deactivated the shield, their fighters can destroy the Death Star.

Han will lead the strike team to Endor with Luke, Leia and Chewbacca. Lando is going to lead the attack on the Death Star. Han lends Lando the *Millennium Falcon,* then sets off for Endor with his strike team.

As Han's strike team lands on Endor, Darth Vader senses that Luke is there. He tells the Emperor, who orders him to go down to Endor and wait for Luke. The Emperor has foreseen that Luke will seek his father out.

On the forest-covered moon, the strike team makes friends with a tribe of Ewoks. Luke tells Leia that she is his twin sister and Darth Vader is their father. Leia is stunned. Luke adds that Darth Vader can sense his presence, and so he must leave the strike team because he is putting them in danger.

Luke surrenders to the Imperial troops and is taken to Darth Vader. He tells the Sith Lord that he has forgotten his true self and

that deep down he is still Anakin Skywalker. Luke can feel the conflict within his father and urges him to let go of his hate. Darth Vader seems thoughtful, but he says that he must obey his master.

The strike team approaches the shield generator. They break in and race to the control room, where they overpower the guards. The *Millennium Falcon* is in position with the Alliance fleet. Everything is going well for the attack. They enter lightspeed and set their course for Endor.

On the Death Star, Darth Vader takes Luke to the Emperor. The Emperor reveals that he knows about the Alliance attack – Luke's friends are walking into a trap. On Endor, Han and the strike team are overpowered by a legion of stormtroopers. When the Alliance fleet comes out of hyperspace, they are attacked by Imperial fighters! They begin to battle for their lives.

From the Death Star, Luke watches the fight in despair. The Emperor tries to encourage Luke to give in to his anger, but Luke refuses, keeping his rage under control.

On Endor, Han and his team are led away by Imperial troops. But suddenly the troops are attacked by the brave little Ewoks! Hundreds rise out of their hiding places in the undergrowth with bows and arrows. A massive battle begins as Leia and Han race back to the shield generator.

The Alliance ships are being destroyed by the overwhelming weapon power of the terrible Death Star. The Alliance commander wants to retreat, but Lando holds his position, trusting Han to deactivate the shield.

The Emperor tells Luke that his Rebellion is lost and his friends will die. He is pleased when he feels Luke's anger because anger leads to the dark side. Luke seizes his lightsaber and turns to strike the Emperor down, but Darth Vader's lightsaber blocks him. The Emperor's triumphant laugh rings through the chamber as Luke and Darth Vader duel.

On Endor, the Ewoks win the battle! The stormtroopers are defeated and Han and Leia rush into the shield generator. Can they destroy it in time?

Luke throws Darth Vader down a flight of steps, then stops as he hears the Emperor chuckle. He rushes away and hides rather than fight his father. But his feelings betray him and Darth Vader senses the existence of Leia at last.

"Obi-Wan was wise to hide her from me," he sneers. "Now his failure is complete."

Luke loses his temper once again. He rushes at Darth Vader with such fury that he knocks him back, and with a furious swipe of his lightsaber he cuts off his father's right hand. The Emperor laughs in delight and encourages Luke to kill his father. But Luke is horrified by what he has done. Turning to face the wicked Emperor, he swears that he will never turn to the dark side.

"I am a Jedi, like my father before me," he says.

"So be it," snarls the Emperor. He turns the full extent of the Force against Luke. Electricity crackles from his fingers, flinging Luke to the ground in agony.

The strike team on Endor detonates the bunker and it explodes, destroying the energy shield. This is Lando's chance! He flies into the heart of the Death Star.

Darth Vader rises to his feet and watches his son writhe on the floor. Luke pleads with him for help. The conflict is wrestling within the Sith Lord, but the Emperor does not notice. At last Darth Vader makes up his mind. He turns to the Emperor, lifts him high into the air and flings him down the power shaft, still crackling with the dark power of the Force that he has generated. The Emperor dies in a terrible explosion of blue lightning. Darth Vader is fatally wounded by the power of the Emperor's evil. He collapses to the floor and Luke rushes to his side.

Elsewhere inside the Death Star, the *Millennium Falcon* locks on to the power generator and hurtles towards it, pursued by Imperial fighters.

Luke carries his father to the landing platform, but the former Jedi Knight is dying. He asks Luke to remove his mask and Luke pulls it off. At last he looks into the face of Anakin Skywalker, white, scarred and hideous. Anakin looks at his son with love, then tells him to go.

"I've got to save you," protests Luke.

"You already have," says Anakin gently. He dies in his son's arms.

On the *Millennium Falcon*, Lando fires on the main power generator and the Death Star begins to explode from within. He escapes just in time and Luke flies out on board a small fighter. The Death Star explodes behind them.

Later that day, across the galaxy, every city and settlement on every planet is celebrating the destruction of the Empire. For a moment, Luke steps away from the celebrations. He sees Yoda and Obi-Wan Kenobi smiling at him. Beside them is a third figure. It is Anakin, but not as he was when Luke saw him last. It is Anakin as he was when he was young, before he turned to the dark side. Luke smiles and rejoins the celebrations, watched by the greatest Jedi Knights of all time.

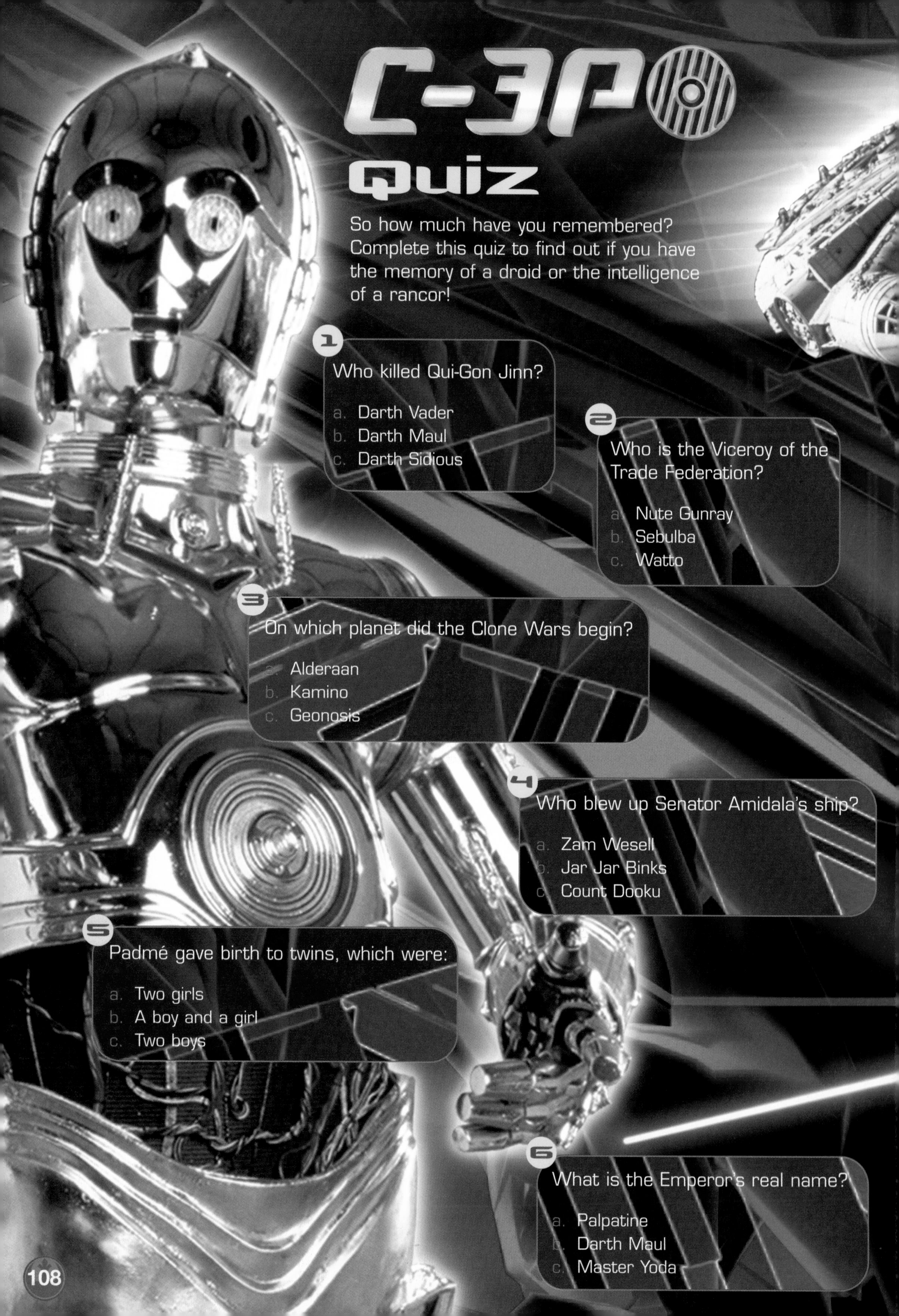

C-3PO
Quiz

So how much have you remembered? Complete this quiz to find out if you have the memory of a droid or the intelligence of a rancor!

1 Who killed Qui-Gon Jinn?

a. Darth Vader
b. Darth Maul
c. Darth Sidious

2 Who is the Viceroy of the Trade Federation?

a. Nute Gunray
b. Sebulba
c. Watto

3 On which planet did the Clone Wars begin?

a. Alderaan
b. Kamino
c. Geonosis

4 Who blew up Senator Amidala's ship?

a. Zam Wesell
b. Jar Jar Binks
c. Count Dooku

5 Padmé gave birth to twins, which were:

a. Two girls
b. A boy and a girl
c. Two boys

6 What is the Emperor's real name?

a. Palpatine
b. Darth Maul
c. Master Yoda

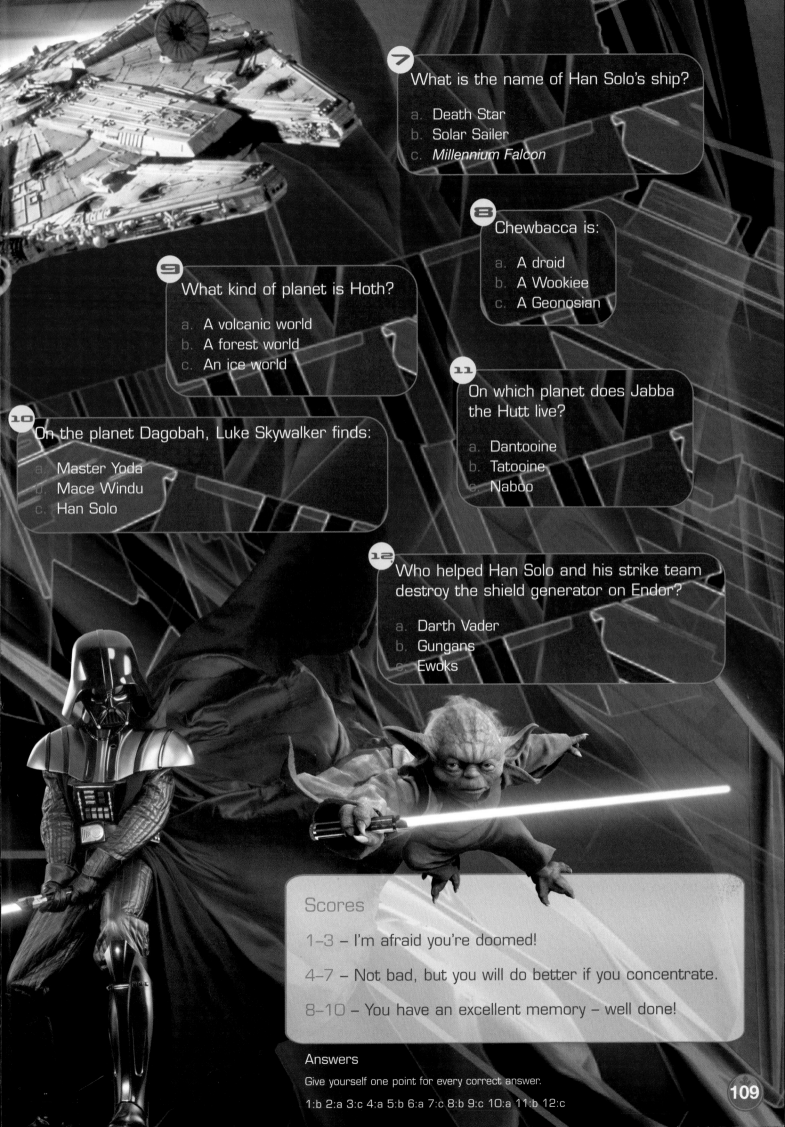

7 What is the name of Han Solo's ship?

a. Death Star
b. Solar Sailer
c. *Millennium Falcon*

8 Chewbacca is:

a. A droid
b. A Wookiee
c. A Geonosian

9 What kind of planet is Hoth?

a. A volcanic world
b. A forest world
c. An ice world

11 On which planet does Jabba the Hutt live?

a. Dantooine
b. Tatooine
c. Naboo

10 On the planet Dagobah, Luke Skywalker finds:

a. Master Yoda
b. Mace Windu
c. Han Solo

12 Who helped Han Solo and his strike team destroy the shield generator on Endor?

a. Darth Vader
b. Gungans
c. Ewoks

Scores

1–3 – I'm afraid you're doomed!

4–7 – Not bad, but you will do better if you concentrate.

8–10 – You have an excellent memory – well done!

Answers

Give yourself one point for every correct answer.

1:b 2:a 3:c 4:a 5:b 6:a 7:c 8:b 9:c 10:a 11:b 12:c

YODA
Jedi Trials

Travelled far you have in your journey to become a Jedi Knight. Take these final trials, then add up your scores to reveal your destiny.

1

What skills do you value most highly inside yourself?

a. Your great strength and fighting skills.
b. Your ability to feel the Force flowing through you.
c. Your ability to move objects with the power of the Force.

2

You have defeated a Jedi who has turned to the dark side and murdered many of your friends. What do you do next?

a. Take him to the Jedi Council to be questioned.
b. Cut him in half with your lightsaber.
c. Ask him to explain his actions to you.

3

You are a talented Padawan and could become a powerful Jedi Knight. How does that make you feel?

a. Proud and strong.
b. Determined to do your best.
c. Afraid that you will not live up to expectations.